More Waterside Walks in the Midlands

by
Birmingham Ramblers

Edited by
Peter Groves

Meridian Books

Published 1998 by Meridian Books.
© Meridian Books 1998
ISBN 1-869922-31-X

A catalogue record for this book is available from the British Library.

The right of Peter Groves to be identified as the editor of this book has been asserted by him in accordance with the Copyright, Designs and Patents Act 1988.

Maps reproduced from the Ordnance Survey mapping with the permission of The Controller of H M S O. © Crown Copyright Licence No. MC 82746M

Publishers' Note

Every care has been taken in the preparation of this book and all the information has been carefully checked and is believed to be correct at the time of publication. However, neither the editor, the authors or the publishers can accept responsibility for any errors or omissions or for any loss, damage, injury or inconvenience resulting from the use of the book.

Meridian Books
40 Hadzor Road
Oldbury
Warley
West Midlands
B68 9LA

Printed in Great Britain by MFP Design & Print, Manchester.

Contents

Location Map

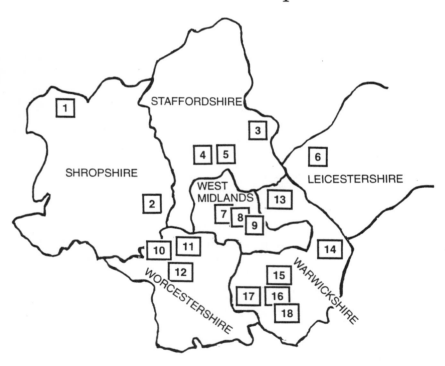

Introduction

IN their first book, *Waterside Walks in the Midlands*, a number of members of the City of Birmingham Branch of the Ramblers' Association co-operated in the preparation a series of walks in some of the Group's favourite walking areas. The Group has now repeated the exercise and I am delighted to be able to present another set on a similar theme.

As before, the walks feature brooks, streams, rivers, canals and pools – sometimes as a major aspect of a walk, sometimes as a feature to encounter as you ramble through some of the fine countryside to which we are so fortunate to have access, virtually on our doorstep. Most of the walks are circular, the three exceptions having ample public transport both at the start and the finish.

Most have long and short versions so you have a choice of distances ranging from 4½ miles/7 km to 14 miles/22.5 km. Counties included are Staffordshire, Shropshire, West Midlands, Leicestershire, Warwickshire and Worcestershire. The three West Midlands walks are centred on Birmingham and demonstrate that the city contains many attractive green areas and watersides.

Some of the authors prefer to give distances in metric units whereas others prefer to use miles and yards. My personal preference is for metric since I find it much easier then to relate to Ordnance Survey maps. However, I have respected the authors' wishes and you will find some local distances in the texts given in yards and some in metres. Since there is little difference in these measurements that is unlikely to cause any problems.

Car parking information is provided and with one exception all of the walks, as I personally have proved, can be reached from Birmingham using public transport. The one exception is the Leicestershire walk and I am grateful to Phil Barnes for taking me out to Snarestone to cover this one.

My thanks also to Des Wright for carefully checking my own contribution to this collection.

I have had a great deal of pleasure in following these walks. I hope that you find them equally rewarding.

Peter Groves

Using this book

ACH walk is accompanied by a sketch map which is designed for guidance but not to replace the relevant Ordnance Survey maps. Even though you may not need to use them O.S. maps are invaluable in case of emergency, bad weather or if for any reason you need to amend your walk. The appropriate numbers of the Landranger (1:50,000) and Pathfinder maps (1:25,000 with much greater detail) are given in the introduction box at the head of each walk. Grid references for the starting points (and the finishing points for the two linear walks) are also given there. If you not sure how to use grid references you will find an explanation on Landranger maps. For the three urban walks the Birmingham A-Z can be very useful.

Always carry a compass, good footwear, adequate waterproofs, a basic first aid kit and some food. We have included information about refreshments, but country pubs are sometimes unable to open at lunchtimes and – sadly – some are forced to close.

Secateurs can sometimes be useful, but even if they are not needed you can help to maintain footpaths by cutting back brambles and vegetation that are starting to intrude.

As has been pointed out in the Introduction all the walks, with the exception of the one in Leicestershire, can be reached by public transport from Birmingham. But routes are sometimes changed and some country services are rather infrequent so always check times and routes with the bus company or British Rail before setting out. Some relevant telephone numbers are given below.

All the walks have been carefully checked but remember that the countryside is continually changing. Footpaths are sometimes diverted or may have become overgrown. They may be ploughed over and not reinstated (as the law requires). Hedges have all too often been destroyed, a process that legislation fortunately has now made less easy. Footbridges may be swept away by floods; river and canal banks may be affected by erosion. We hope that you will not be affected by any of these problems but if you are the publishers would be pleased to have details. Illegal footpath obstructions should be reported to the local authority.

Useful telephone numbers:

British Rail	0345 484950	Shropshire Busline	0345 056785
Centro (West Midlands)	0121 200 2700	Staffordshire Busline	01785 223344
Worcestershire Busline	0345 125436	Warwickshire Transport	01926 412135
Leicestershire Busline	0116 2511411		

Abbreviations: TWM Travel West Midlands; MRW Midland Red West

1
The Meres and Canal Around Ellesmere

by Horace Marsh

A circular walk embracing the Meres, the Llangollen Canal and the lovely North Shropshire countryside, starting and finishing at the Visitors Centre on the foreshore of the Mere alongside the A528 on the outskirts of the charming North Shropshire town of Ellesmere.

Distance: 9 miles (14.5 km).
Maps: Landranger 126; Pathfinder 828.
Car Parking: Opposite the Visitor Centre and along the A528 and in the centre of Ellesmere (GR406346).
Public Transport: British Rail to Gobowen or National Express coaches to Oswestry then Midland Red Shropshire Bus D53 to Ellesmere. Alight in Cross Street, go back along Cross Street to 'The Railway' and take the path on the opposite side of the street. Go through the car park and turn right along Church Street to pass the parish church and reach the Mere. Turn left through the black gates of Cremorn Gardens. *Now start reading from the second sentence of the first paragraph.*
Start/Finish: Visitors Centre on A528 (GR406346).
Refreshments: Sun Inn, Welshampton; Pubs and shops in Ellesmere

! The complete walk goes through a short canal tunnel towards the end of the walk. This is only 80 metres long, is quite straight and has a stout handrail on the canal side. It can be walked without difficulty but it is dark so you may wish to carry a torch.

STARTING from the Visitor Centre walk along the shore of the Mere towards Ellesmere for about 200 metres to the black gates of the Cremorn Gardens. Go through these and follow the path, continuously bearing right, around the western, northern and eastern shores of the Mere. The path runs through a wooded foreshore with a variety of trees some of which are fitted with nesting boxes. There is a wide variety of birdlife on or around the Mere including tufted duck, great crested grebe, mallard, Canada geese, herons on the island, gulls, warblers, snipe, curlew and lapwing.

At the third stile on the eastern shore a field will be reached: cross the stile and turn immediately left keeping the fence and hedgerow on the

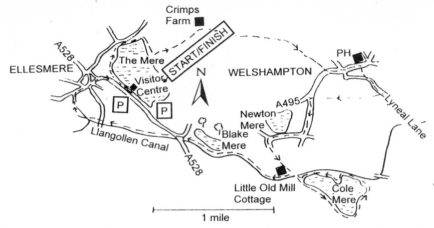

left. Cross two stiles and continue walking alongside the hedge through a small wooded area to a third stile. After crossing this turn away from the hedge and walk diagonally left towards a gap in the far wire fence in the direction of Crimps Farm which will be seen directly in front. After going through the gap walk diagonally ahead to a stile in the wooden fence bordering a farm track. Cross over this stile and walk up the farm track opposite, ignoring a gate into the field on the right hand side. After walking along this track for about 100 metres two field gates will be encountered: go through the gate on the left and carry on along the track.

At the end of the track go through the field gate and walk directly ahead uphill and over the crest to a stile in the wire fence. At the stile look to the left to see a derelict house, and if the weather conditions are reasonably clear it will be rewarding to take a backward look to obtain a panoramic view of both the Ruabon Mountain and the Berwyn mountains: in winter these will often be snow dusted or snow covered.

Cross the stile and walk downhill across the field towards the right hand end of a row of trees ahead. These trees were formerly a part of Lea Wood. At this point a stile in the wire fence will be met. Cross the stile and turn right, following the fence on the right until a stile is encountered. Cross the stile and walk diagonally across the corner of the field to a further stile in a wire fence. Cross this stile and walk directly ahead across the centre of the field, and up a slight rise, in line with a large tree, seen on the left of two smaller trees. Walk just beyond this tree, which is growing in the hedge on the right, to the end of the field.

Cross a stile beside a gate and walk with the hedge on the right to reach a hedge corner. Turn right at this corner and walk diagonally to the left of a large oak tree to skirt a small depression which in wet weather may be partially filled with water to make a small pool.

When the hedge (+fence) is shortly rejoined walk along the left-hand side of this until a stile is reached, shortly after passing a small pool on the other side of the fence. Cross the stile and walk down the right-hand side of the hedge (on the left-hand side of the field) until a field gate is encountered. Go through this gate onto a farm track.

Turn right along this track and walk to the end where a farm gate will be met. Go through this gate and cross the farmyard to walk out through the farm entrance on to the main A495 road to Whitchurch. Turn left and walk along the footpath into Welshampton as far as the Sun Inn passing the Church of St Michaels and All Angels on the way.

The Sun Inn is an ideal hostelry for a refreshment stop since walkers are welcome, a wide range of bar snacks, main meals, sweets, sandwiches, tea, coffee along with a number of draught beers and cider, are all served in a comfortable lounge. On Sundays a traditional Sunday lunch is also served. The inn was built about 1770 as a farm and later converted to a malting house.

On leaving the Sun Inn cross over the A495 road towards a service station on the right to locate the public footpath sign denoting the path running down the opening between the left hand side of the garage and the right hand side of a terrace of houses.

Walk down the path and cross two stiles to gain Lyneal Lane which runs between Lyneal and Welshampton. Turn left and walk along the lane for about 300 metres where a stile in the hedge on the right hand side of the lane will be met just prior to the large redbrick gatehouse of Lyneal Lodge. Cross the stile and follow the fence bordering the grounds of Lyneal Lodge until a stile is encountered. Cross the stile and continue to walk diagonally across the field sighting on a large tree on the extreme right of a number of trees in the middle distance, beyond the crest of a small hillock in the immediate foreground.

Having walked over the crest of this hillock it will be seen that the tree is adjacent to a circular concrete water tank in the next field. The line of the path to be walked is between the tank and the tree; however, because the path is obstructed along this line of the path by the hedge you will probably need to divert a little to the right to walk through the large gap in the furthermost right hand corner of the field (left of a protruding hedge corner), which was probably previously a field gate, to gain access into the next field.

Swing left to regain the original line of the path and walk between the tree and the water tank, then veer slightly to the right after the tank to a small gap in the hedge (probably an old stile site). Walk through this gap and, keeping to the line, cross the field to a gap in the far right hand corner of the far hedge. Go through the gap and walk straight ahead, then downhill to a small gate and stile in the hedge on the far side of the field. Go through the gate and walk diagonally to a stile and gateway in the right hand corner of the field into a lane running between the A495 and Colemere.

Turn left along the lane towards Colemere and walk to a cross roads, turn right at the cross roads and walk up the lane past Newton Mere on the right turning left at the end of the Mere onto a wide footpath on the left hand side of the lane. Walk up the footpath, hedged on both sides, swinging left after about 50 metres. Soon losing the left-hand hedge, continue forward with the hedge on the right.

Turn left at the end of the field when a plantation of newly planted trees is reached. Walk along the front edge of the plantation almost to the far left hand side of the field where, approximately 50 metres beyond a large single oak tree, the somewhat overgrown path turns diagonally to the right to a gap in the corner of the field leading to the canal bridge over the Llangollen Canal. Cross the bridge pausing to admire the beautiful old cottage on the right named the 'Little Old Mill'. Pass the cottage and walk through a kissing gate on the left hand side of the lane marked 'Boathouse Wood'. This path follows the southern side of Cole Mere through the lovely wooded foreshore to the far end of the Mere. After going through the gate at the Sailing Club follow the path to the end of the club enclosure turning left at the eastern end of the Mere past the fenced yacht park to a stile and a kissing gate. Go through the gate and walk across the grassy foreshore at the end of the Mere to a further kissing gate marked 'Yell Wood' on the opposite northern side of the Mere. Follow the attractive path meandering through the wood finally climbing up some steps to emerge alongside the Llangollen Canal.

Walk along this elevated pleasant path between the Mere and the canal passing the first Bridge No. 54, continue along the path to the lane opposite the Little Old Mill cottage. Turn right and walk along the lane to cross over the canal bridge, then turning left, immediately drop down on to the canal towpath and walk westwards in the same direction towards Ellesmere.

After walking 200 metres or so beyond Bridge 56 Blake Mere will be reached, this small Mere is surrounded by woods and is a popular spot for anglers. Just beyond the end of the Mere the towpath reaches a road tunnel running under the A495.

At this point, if you are travelling by car, you have the choice of continuing for the complete walk or choosing a shorter route back to the Visitors Centre car park. For the complete walk now continue reading from ✶ below.

4

To return to the Visitors Centre you have two options:

1) Leave the towpath by climbing the exit up to the road, then after crossing the A495 walk down the footpath on the right hand side towards Ellesmere to the Visitors Centre, where the walk ends.

2) Alternatively, to reduce road walking, go through the tunnel and along the towpath for about 350 metres until a stile in the hedge is reached. Cross the stile and walk along the left hand side of the hedge to its end where a further stile will be encountered in the wire fence. Cross the stile and walk along the left hand side of the hedge, which borders the grounds of the Catholic Church, to the stile on the edge of the main road. Cross the stile, and then cross over the A528 main road, turn left and walk down the footpath on the right hand side of the road to the Visitors Centre to complete the walk.

* For the complete walk follow the canal through the tunnel and continue on along the towpath for just over a kilometre until a road bridge is reached. Go under the bridge, continue forward and turn right at the junction with the Ellesmere spur, then cross the footbridge over the spur to the towpath on the opposite side and walk the short distance to the wharf which is virtually in the centre of Ellesmere. Here there are several hostelries and one or two teashops offering refreshments, and also the town and the Parish Church of the Blessed Virgin Mary are well worth exploration.

Wharf Road will take you from the wharf into the town. Turn right along Scotland Street, then left along Cross Street. To return to the Visitor Centre walk along Cross Street as far as 'The Railway' and take the path on the opposite side of the street. Go through the car park and turn right along Church Street to pass the parish church and reach the Mere, then walk along the footpath on the left hand side of the A528 to the Visitors Centre to end the walk.

For the bus continue along Cross Street, past 'The Railway', to meet the bus stop on the left.

2
Alveley and the River Severn

by Sylvia and Harry Hickman

Distance: 8½ miles (13.5 km)
Maps: Landranger 138; Pathfinder 932
Car Parking: Severn Valley Visitor Centre (GR753839) – this is situated just outside the village of Alveley and is signposted from the A442 Birmingham to Kidderminster Road.
Public Transport: Bus service 297 (Kidderminster/Bridgnorth). Alight at Alveley County School and then follow the walk from ✳ on page 7
Steam Train (adds one mile but makes a very interesting addition to the walk): Severn Valley Railway to Highley station. From the station drop down to the River Severn, turn left and walk for half a mile to reach the Miners Bridge. Cross this, turn left and then continue reading from ❍ below.
Start/Finish: Severn Valley Visitor Centre (GR753839)
Refreshments: Pubs at Hampton Loade and Alveley

ROM the Visitor Centre walk down the hill to the River Severn. The bridge across the river is the Miners Bridge (so called because it was originally the link between two pits, at Highley and Alveley – do not use it but turn right over the stile so that the river is on your left.

❍ Follow the river, crossing several stiles. Keeping a large house and garden on the left cross a narrow lane, then walk through more fields until you see a white building – the Lion Inn – to your right. Leave the field by the left corner stile and turn right for 50 yds towards the Lion Inn, then turn left into Hampton Loade.

Pass Ferry Cottage on your left and take the signposted path on the right through a garden, climbing a stile, then going forward to cross another stile to the left of a wooden shed. Go up the slope and forward across a field keeping to the left of a pylon and walking under the power lines. When you reach a single barbed wire fence with a protective cover (*you may have to negotiate an electric fence to reach this*) cross this, turn right and follow the fence round, keeping the barbed wire, then some wood-land, on your right-hand side. (*The path in this field has been realigned as the result of a diversion order. The OS maps show it running beside a wood on*

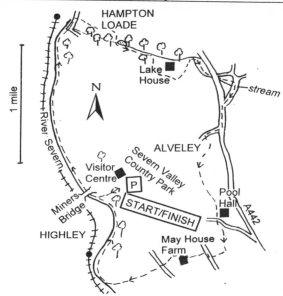

the left-hand side of the field. At the time of writing the barbed wire fence had a rather temporary appearance so some changes might be possible here.) Reaching a stile in the right-hand corner of the field, cross this and turn right onto a track.

After about 20 yds down the track turn right through a gate and follow the path through the wood to a footbridge by a small waterfall. Climb the path for 50 yds and turn left by a footpath sign. Follow the path, with the stream on your left, through a wood. Cross a footbridge, then bear right up the hill, ignoring another footbridge on the left. Cross a stile and turn right, then keeping a hedge and a wood on the right-hand side go through two fields, and in the second field cross a stile in the hedge and go down rough steps to reach a track. Turn left along this, then right at a T-junction. About 80 yds further on turn left into a field with a hedge on the left.

Climb a stile and drop down the hillside, bearing right to a corner stile. Keeping a stream on the left, and passing a waterwheel, cross a bridge and follow a track to a T-junction. Turn right and walk to the A442. Cross this and take the signposted path opposite (to the right of a lane). Cross the field to its far right-hand corner and turn right into a road, bear right at the road junction to the A442. Turn left to reach the Squirrel pub on the right-hand side.

Pass a garage on the left and turn into the next road on the right. Pass the playing fields on the left.

∗ *Start here if you are travelling by bus.*

Take the path that runs between the school and the playing fields. When you reach a road turn left and almost opposite is a signposted path. Cross a footbridge into a field and go forward along the path with bushes on the left. Cross a stile and in the next field bear slightly right to a big oak tree and to a stile on the right.

After the stile keep the hedge on the left-hand side for two fields, then cross a field keeping the same line and crossing several stiles to reach a farm drive with a fence on the right-hand side.

Walk down the farm drive to a road and cross this into the field opposite (poor stile, no waymarking) keeping a hedge on the left. Go through a gate with a hedge on the left. At the end of the second field turn right, with a hedge still on the left, and go through a gate into a lane. Turn right and after 50 yds turn left down a farm drive. Turn right in front of a metal barn to a stile, then keeping a fence on the left walk to the bottom of the field and cross a stile on the left. In the next field keep the hedge on the right and after about 100yds reach a stile on the right. Cross this and keeping the hedge initially on the left-hand side maintain the line of the path to reach a stile into a lane.

Cross the lane to a footpath opposite. Keeping the hedge on the right-hand side go through three gateways to reach a ruined building (Nether Hollies). Drop down to the river, turn right and follow the river back to the Miners Bridge.

If you have come on the train now cross the bridge, turn left and return to the station.

If you have come by bus, continue reading from ○ on page 6

Otherwise turn right and make your way back to the Severn Valley County Park.

3

Barton-under-Needwood and the Trent & Mersey Canal

by Heinke Jenkins

A walk through some attractive Staffordshire countryside to Battlestead Hill, returning along the Trent & Mersey Canal, with an opportunity to visit Branston Water Park.

Distance: 11 miles (17.5 km) (plus any additional walking that you may care to do around Branston Water Park).
Maps: Landranger 128; Pathfinder 851/852.
Car Parking: Near St James Church, Barton-under-Needwood on the B5016.
Public Transport: Bus; Stephenson's 112 (Birmingham/Lichfield/Barton/Burton). Alight at Barton Turn on the A38(T) and walk about three-quarters of a mile into Barton-under-Needwood.
Start/Finish: Barton-under-Needwood (GR187186).
Refreshments: Pubs at Shrobnal and just past Branston Lock.

! The Trent & Mersey Canal in part follows the busy A38(T). To avoid traffic noise this walk is best done at a weekend or public holiday.

FROM St James' church walk to the High Street (B5016) and turn left on it, cross the road and follow it for a quarter of a mile. At a sign to the Catholic church watch out on your right for a house named 'The Limes', next to which is a bridlepath. Turn into the gravelled path with 'The Limes' on your right and go through a gate. Ahead you will see a stile leading into a field (ignore the stile on your right). Cross the stile into the field and follow the fence on your right (signed Dunstall). Cross another stile and go straight ahead at a cross-roads of paths. Cross a stile beside a gate and follow the tree lined path, then go through another gate into a field.

Follow the hedge on your left, going through a small wood and crossing a stile to soon approach another wooded area on your left. After passing under power lines and just past three large mature trees on your right you will see a sliding gate on your left between the hedge. This leads to a *secret lake* in the woods with lots of water fowl on it. There are also some ancient acacia trees in this little wood. *Although clearly well used, the path to the lake is not a right of way.*

Now continue on in a northerly direction. Soon, on your left you will get glimpses of Dunstall church. Ahead of you a gate and stile lead into a minor road. Cross the stile and turn left on the road, soon to pass Dunstall cricket ground on your right and with views through the trees to Dunstall Hall. Reaching a crossing keep straight ahead to pass Dunstall church on your left. This farm road leads, in about a quarter of a mile, to Spinks Barn Farm. When you approach the farm go through the gate to your right onto a pleasant green lane with some attractive views.

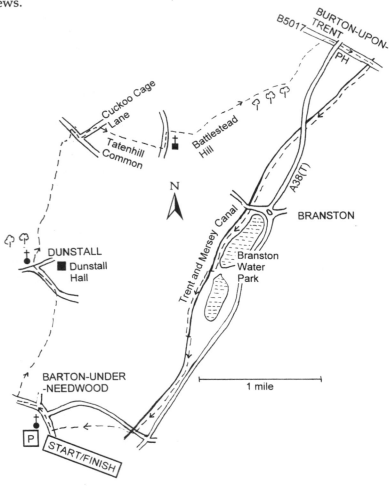

10

After going through three more gates you will enter a large field with Highlands Park Farm on the horizon. Walk through the middle of the field towards the farm, go through a metal gate and follow the farm track through the tidy farm. Continue forward, now along a surfaced drive, until you reach a T-junction with a minor road. Turn right along it and walk on until you see a phone box on your right. Cross the road and turn left into the delightfully named Cuckoo Cage Lane. After reaching the second house on the left (Rockets Oak) turn right along a signed bridle-way. Go through two gates to arrive at an open and breathtaking view of rolling countryside. This is Tatenhill Common.

Go forward through a field, swinging slightly left and making for a gate in the hedge ahead of you. You will soon see Burton power station, the Trent & Mersey Canal and Branston Water Park. Go through the gate and follow the hedge on your left. After another gate you will arrive at a sheep meadow and, in the dip, surrounded by trees on your right, you will make out Tatenhill church. Follow on along the hedge on your left, down the dip and through a gate onto a road. Turn left, passing some lovely houses.

Watch out for a footpath sign and stile just past Rose Cottage on your right. To the left of the gate, beside a seat, you will see Tatenhill's ancient well. Go over the stile, then leaving the house to your right and a field fence to your left, go roughly south-east to climb a path up Battlestead Hill. At the top take a breather and look back in the direction from which you have come.

When you have your breath back make for the hedge at the top of the hill. Cross a stile in the top left corner of the field and walk in a north-easterly direction, keeping the hedge on your right. After crossing four closely spaced stiles cross a little plank bridge over a ditch, then over a stile to the other side of the hedge. Follow this hedge, now on your left, until it bends to the right where, in a gap in the hedge, you will see a stile. Cross this, followed shortly by another, to arrive in a large field with wide views to your right and a hedge to your left.

Follow this hedge and fence until you see a gap, then cross onto a hard-core farm track and follow this to the farm, with a hedge initially on the right. As you approach the farm buildings look out for a footpath sign in a hedge corner on your left. Cross a double stile and follow the hedge on your right. Just left of the far corner of the field you will meet a double gate and a footbridge. Go through, cross a stile and again go towards the now reappearing farm track on your right. Now you will pass on your right the sad remains of an old Elizabethan farm. This is Sinai Park Farm and 'The Lord's Well'; it has seen better times! Once it was worked by monks; now a new owner has been found and one hopes that it will be saved.

Continue forward to pass a solitary house on your right and now, instead of following the little road towards the left, step onto the grassy area in front of you, keeping the tall bushes on your left and the house to your right. Go down this steep meadow and catch up again with the tarmac path down below. Crossing a cattle grid and bridge spanning a little brook you will soon come to a road junction with the B5017. Turn sharp right along this road – you are now in Shrobnal.

Pass St Aidan's church on your right and, before you go under the bridge carrying the A38, you will see the Albion pub – a good lunch stop.

Freshly strengthened, go under the bridge to pass Marston's brewery and many nicely renovated brewery terraced houses. Soon you are on the canal bridge; turn right down some steps past Shrobnal Marina and walk along the towpath of the Trent & Mersey Canal. This canal was built by James Brindley between 1766 and 1777 and was used mainly for transporting goods and raw materials to and from the Potteries. It is 92 miles long and runs from Shardlow, on the River Trent, to Preston Brook, near Runcorn. As you walk along it look out for the fine iron mileposts dated 1819 which you can use to check the distance you are walking – you will leave the canal shortly after passing the milepost marked Shardlow 20, Preston Brook 72.

In about 1¼ miles you will reach Branston Lock with its overflow on your left and soon the Bridge Inn (another refreshing stop!) with colourful boats moored outside. After about 100 yards you will reach Branston Water Park. Here you can either walk through the park (parallel to the canal) or keep on along the towpath. There are lots of picnic benches in the park and many waterfowl to see. You can also go for a stroll around the lake, one of several left from gravel extraction.

Continue along the towpath until you reach bridge 35 and Tatenhill Lock. Stand on the bridge and look back over the extensive park with lakes on both sides of the canal.

You now change sides on the canal until reaching the next bridge where you then cross back again. On the left side of the canal you can see extensive brickworks; on the right meadows and, later, gravel works.

At bridge 38 (don't be misled by bridge 37A!) you are at Barton Turn. Go over the bridge on the B5016, noticing the handsome wharf houses on your right. Ahead you can now see Barton-under-Needwood. Walk about 50 yards and look on the left for a footpath sign. Only three quarters of a mile to Barton now! Cross over and enter the short surfaced drive, to be faced with an iron gate leading to the sewage works. Turn

Branston Water Park

sharp right to walk between a fence and a little stream, passing some metal sheds.

Cross a stile leading to a field and extensive gravel works. Continue forward, soon crossing a new road (*not on the OS map*) via stiles, always with the stream on your right. Then, look out for a little bridge over the stream and a stile on your right. Cross the stile and turn left along the hedge to an open green. Watch out for a bridge on the left at the end of the green. Cross this to enter another narrower green: turn right on it and at the end of this green you will meet a gate and stile. Cross the stile onto a little road and continue forward, passing the village pond on your left and some pretty houses, and the stream again, on your right.

Soon you will see the main road and a brick bridge over the stream with a stile. Climb this and turn right onto the road, Efflinch Lane. Walk forward until you come to a T-junction with the main road, the B5016. Turn sharp left on this and in a few minutes you will see your starting point of St James' Church.

4
Twice Brewood

by Trevor Antill

Following both the Staffordshire & Worcestershire and the Shropshire Union canals this walk follows waterways from differing eras. The Staffs & Worcs, built by James Brindley and opened in 1772, is one of the oldest and most attractive waterways in the country. It owes much of this beauty to its meandering, contour route which enabled Brindley to avoid cuttings, embankments and; where possible; locks. By contrast, in 1835, when the Shropshire Union was opened, the expertise in soil mechanics had improved enormously – though not completely as the famous Thomas Telford (who didn't live to see the canal opened) discovered to his cost at nearby Shelmore. The result is that the second canal you follow takes a direct line along steep embankments and deep cuttings.

Brewood (pronounced Brewed) is a large village which started life as a Roman camp located to guard the nearby (A5) Watling Street. Situated in a Royal Forest and often frequented by Norman royalty it later evolved into a flourishing medieval market town. Containing several buildings of architectural interest perhaps the most unusual is Speedwell Castle, a large Georgian Gothic house, said to have been built from the winnings of a racehorse named 'Speedwell'.

Distance: 13½ miles (21.5 km) or 9 miles (14.5 km). The shorter walk uses public transport to return to Brewood or Wolverhampton.
Maps: Landranger 127; Pathfinder 871/891.
Car Parking: Public car park (Stafford Street) in Brewood. Lay-bys on A5 near Gailey Wharf.
Public Transport: Green Bus service 2/3 from Wolverhampton.
Start/Finish: Brewood centre (GR883087).
Refreshments: Tea-shop and pubs in Brewood; pub at Cross Green.

FROM the centre of Brewood walk south-east along Sandy Lane. Passing Vicarage Road on the left arrive at 'The Pavement' where you go left and, ignoring a footpath right, follow the lane to bear right over a stream bridge. Ignoring the first public footpath sign immediately on the left continue with the lane for a short distance to a Y-junction where another public footpath sign points left. Go left with it and so enter an unsurfaced green lane to soon meet a gated step stile.

Over this go forward with the hedge/fence on your right and in the next corner cross a step stile. Walk forward a few yards, with the hedge now on your left, to the remains of a step stile and so forward along a field edge still with the hedge left. In about 200 yards swing diagonally right across the field to a hedge gap and so onto a lane.

Go left along the lane and follow it to a junction coming in from the right. Turn just a few feet into the junction and on the left you will find an old public footpath sign which takes you over a broken fence stile and into a field corner. Now crossing the centre of the field aim for the farmhouse opposite where you will come to a step stile. Over this go forward again to pass immediately left of the farmhouse and so cross two footbridges in quick succession – the second one taking you over the River Penk. Continue forward with the left-hand fence to pass a house and soon reach a corner and a step stile. Cross this into a hedged drive/lane and go forward to meet a road.

At this point you are on the very edge of Somerford Park.

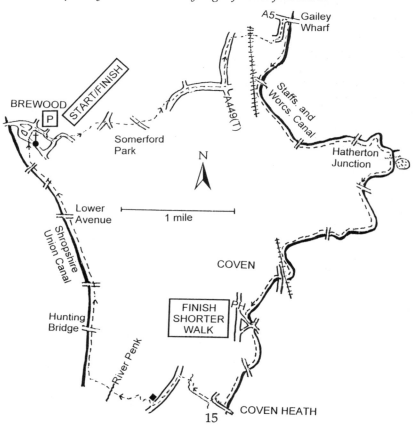

Cross the road to the signed step stile opposite and in the field walk slightly right of forward across to the opposite hedgerow (bearing 75 degrees) where there is a hedge gap just left of an oak tree. Through the gap and in the next field walk across it diagonally left to another large oak tree near the corner and next to a lane (bearing 40 degrees). At the gap join the lane to follow it left all the way to the busy A449 dual carriageway.

Carefully cross to the other side of the dual carriageway and go left to follow its pavement north. In about a third of a mile you will see a red 'Reduce Speed Now' sign in the central reservation: immediately after this there is a public footpath sign and a hedge gap on the right. Having reduced your speed (!) go right through the hedge gap and walk across the field, very slightly left of forward, to the brick bridge that crosses a railway. In the next field go diagonally right (120 degrees) across and aiming just right of the house partially hidden by trees. This will bring you to the right protruding corner of its garden where you continue forward to follow the edge of the field with the fence on your left so passing right of the house. Keep following the edge of the field to meet a crossing hedgerow where you go left to join a surfaced lane. Go right and follow the lane to houses and the canal where you then follow the lane as it swings left to arrive at the A5 Watling Street.

Here go right onto the Staffordshire & Worcestershire Canal to follow the towpath south (if the gate to the canal is closed you will have to cross the A5, take the steps down to the canal and go under the A5). *You are here at Gailey top lock where the 'Round House', now a canal shop, was originally the lock keeper's watchtower, giving a good view of approaching boats.*

After a while the towpath will take you through chemical works – not quite as bad as it sounds – and after a further while will bring you to Hatherton Junction.

At this junction there is a marina with a shop and other facilities. The former Hatherton branch of the Staffs & Worcs used to leave here to join with the BCN but it has been closed for many years. A very short distance further along your route the towpath aqueducts over a stream where, on the opposite side of the canal, is a curious, yet attractive, moated island. Not being able to find out much about it I can only presume it serves an ornamental purpose.

From the junction follow the fingerpost sign for Wolverhampton and Stourport. Now stay with this meandering towpath for the next four miles, passing The Anchor pub on the way.

To shorten the walk you can leave the canal by the fishermen's path immediately after bridge 70, then go right to the A449. The Green Bus, service 2/3 runs along here between Wolverhampton and Brewood.

16

Otherwise continue along the towpath until reaching Coven Heath bridge number 69. At the bridge leave the canal to go right (north-west) along the lane.

Soon, at a sharp right bend in the lane, go left through a gate and follow the signed bridleway along the roughly surfaced lane for about 50 yards to reach a bridged stream. Immediately before the bridge there is a step stile on the right which you cross into the field corner to walk forward along the edge with the stream and levee on your left. Follow both around a right bend and stay with the levee until, just past a line of mid-field oak trees; you arrive at an easily missed gap on the left. Go through and over a bridge to pass left of a young plantation and so arrive at a step stile. At the time of writing the plantation was rather overgrown – you are aiming here for the field on your left. Cross into a field and walk forward with the right hedge to the double gates in front at a road.

On the road go left and follow it for about a third of a mile until arriving at a junction and houses on the right – just before the motorway bridge (not yet visible, but audible!). Here go right and follow the concrete road forward to pass left of the houses and so arrive at a large rectangular area of concrete – the site of the former Lower Pendeford Farm. Turn left to follow the concrete track for about 50 yards through two gateways to a hedgerow. The now unsurfaced track swings right to a barn and then left between fields to gently descend to a bridge over the River Penk. On the other side of the bridge stay with the track to pass

The elegant Avenue Bridge over the Shropshire Union Canal

a derelict house and so reach a crossing track and the canal towpath fence - the Shropshire Union Canal.

At the fence you may be able to go through a gap where you turn right along the towpath. If this is not possible go right to follow the unsurfaced track – a bridleway – adjacent and parallel to the towpath. Arriving at the first canal bridge (number 7) leave the bridleway to join the towpath and follow it north. This bridge (Hunting Bridge) brings the Monarch's Way (a long distance path following the route taken by Charles II after his defeat by Cromwell's forces at the Battle of Worcester) from Chillington onto the canal. After a while you will pass under the high and elegant, balustraded Avenue Bridge (bridge 10) which takes Chillington Hall's ornamental drive over the canal.

Passing through a steep cutting you will eventually arrive at bridge 12. Immediately after passing under this bridge leave the canal by taking the step stile on the right into a field. Walking diagonally left on a rough line for the church steeple, cross the field and a small brick bridge to continue forward with the fence on your right and so over another step stile. Forward again, now with a hedge on your right, will bring you to the top corner and over a stile onto an unsurfaced lane. Here go left and then immediately right into an enclosed footpath. Follow this to emerge at a road in front of Brewood church. Go left and then right to follow Church Road back into the centre of Brewood.

5
The Sherbrook Valley
by Heinke Jenkins

This is a very varied walk, going through woods along the Sherbrook Valley, perhaps spotting some deer!; then along the colourful and busy Trent & Mersey Canal with pastures and the River Trent for company. The walk returns to the starting point passing through the impressive Shugborough Estate with its Hall, various follies and cattle meadows.

> **Distance:** 10 miles (16 km).
> **Maps:** Landranger 127, 128; Pathfinder 850, 851, 871.
> **Car Parking:** Commonwealth War Cemetery, Cannock Chase (GR983155).
> **Public Transport:** Bus or train to Hednesford, then Midland Red North 25/26 circular or 832 to Pye Green Corner. From Pye Green Corner walk north along Broadhurst Green (towards the BT tower), go over the crossroads and continue forward (signed Katyn Memorial) for about 100 yards to reach the Commonwealth War Cemetery.
> **Start/Finish:** Cannock Chase Commonwealth War Cemetery (GR983155).
> **Refreshments:** Lock House Restaurant; Clifford Arms, Great Haywood.

F ROM the cemetery car park follow the track ahead of you in a northerly direction, shortly passing the well kept German Military Cemetery. Soon the track becomes wood lined; after a while it opens up on the left-hand side with views over the heath, and you pass a post signed 'Springslade'. Approaching a crossing track, your track splits into two; take the left-hand one, passing a post pointing to the Stepping Stones. You are still keeping the woods to the right of you, but almost immediately on your right is the Sher Brook, a little stream that will accompany you until you reach the Stepping Stones in about two miles.

When you reach a point where the track swings round left in a semi-circle do not be tempted to continue forward on a path leading across a tiny stream. This path has been diverted to preserve the wetlands across which it passes. However, at the time of writing the diversion notice was missing. Just continue along the track which soon swings back along your original course.

A little further on you reach a grassy area on your right and the Sher Brook widens into a nice basin. Continue straight ahead (signed Staffs

Way), the Sher Brook collecting into a winding little stream on your right, until, after about 1½ miles, you reach the Stepping Stones which you step over. There are picnic benches here, if you feel like a rest. Now follow on straight ahead (ignoring the grassy path on your right) and changing direction to the east. On your left you now have a wire fence and ever so often you will see fascinating ancient oaks with enormous girths. These remain from the original Cannock Chase forest, before it was 'developed' by the Forestry Commission.

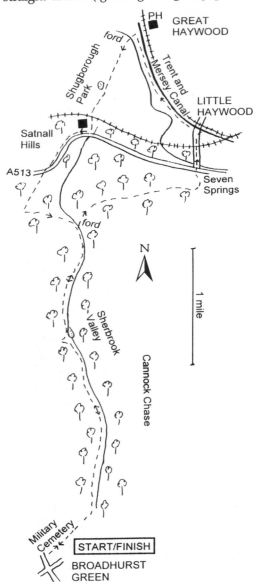

The land soon opens up on your right to some steep rising ground, Haywood Warren. Ignore branches off and, keeping to the main track you soon arrive at Seven Springs car park. Keep to the left of the car park and you will see a track becoming a tarmac lane. Watch out for cars now! At the bottom of the lane you reach a T-junction with the A51. Cross the road, over Weetman's Bridge which spans the Trent. Follow this minor road, soon under a railway bridge: before the next bridge, you will see the Trent & Mersey Canal before you. Watch out for the footpath sign on your right; walk down some steps by the canal, turn left under the bridge and walk along the canal to Great Haywood.

As you walk along the canal you soon see on your left, over the meadows, Shugborough Hall. Pass under a pretty black and white iron bridge and then, at the next bridge, leave the canal. Walk over the bridge and on your left you will see the entrance to the Lock House Restaurant, a very good lunch stop. You can sit outside and watch the boats struggling through the lock, or inside in the cosy dining room. For the Clifford Arms pub go a few yards further, under the bridge.

Retrace your steps over the bridge and head for the ancient Essex Bridge which spans the River Trent in front of you. Follow the tarmac track through the Shugborough Estate, past the Hall itself, then pastures, a folly (the Tower of the Winds) and Shugborough Farm, all on your left, and a garden centre on your right. After crossing a railway bridge you may spot another folly over to the right.

Soon the tarmac track bends to the right; you take the path through the wood immediately in front of you to reach the A51. Turn right along here for about half a mile until the road bends to the right. Then cross the road and make towards the woodland path on your left – you will probably see cars parked there.

You are now on the Staffordshire Way. Stay on the main path ahead of you for about a quarter of a mile until you come to a T-junction in the path. Here take a sharp left turn until you see the Stepping Stones that you passed earlier. Now follow the path ahead of you (do not cross over the stepping stones) and follow the Sher Brook back to the Commonwealth Cemetery.

The Stepping Stones

21

6

By the Ashby Canal

by Phil Barnes and John Penny

This circular walk takes you through a quiet, unsung, yet agreeably pastoral corner of west Leicestershire, close to the Warwickshire border. It includes a lock-free section of the Ashby Canal, three attractive, unassuming villages, each boasting welcoming pubs, woodland stretches, farmland and the northern terminus, complete with nineteenth century railway architecture, of the Battlefield Line.

Its length makes it ideal for a half day walk, or a midday one, allowing you to lunch in one of the pubs or the tea-room at Shackerstone station. Alternatively, it makes an ideal leg stretcher for a fine summer evening.

Route-finding through the fields during the first half of the walk is greatly assisted by excellent waymarking. Stiles are in good condition throughout. The final section along the canal presents no route finding difficulties whatsoever.

Distance: 7 miles (11 km).
Maps: Landranger 140; Pathfinder 893.
Car Parking: Roadside in Snarestone's main street, close to the Globe pub (GR343093).
Public Transport: None suitable. However, a possibility is to catch the Battlefield Line train from Market Bosworth or Shenton to the terminus at Shackerstone, then pick up the walk from there. N.B. This is a very limited service so check timetables! (tel 01827-880754).
Start/Finish: Snarestone (GR343093).
Refreshments: Pubs at Snarestone, Newton Burgoland and Shackerstone; tea-room at Shackerstone station (limited opening times).

WALK eastwards along the right-hand side of the village's main street for 250m, observing some fine late eighteenth century houses on both sides. Look out for the village War Memorial which is set back from the road on your right hand side. Immediately after the War Memorial, turn right along a track. After 30m, look out for a stile on your left signed 'Ivanhoe Way'.

Cross this stile into the field and walk diagonally to the next stile: cross into the next field and head for the waymarked stile on the opposite side of this field, left of a hedge corner. Proceed in a south easterly direction across fields for about a further 600m, keeping the

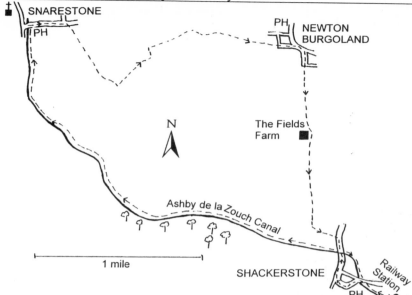

hedge on your right and using the regularly-spaced fingerposts to guide you.

Towards the end of this section, you will pass a small copse on your right surrounding a secluded pool. At the end of the field, pass through a gap in the hedge and over a ditch crossed by a narrow bridge. You will then be on an unmade farm track with a stretch of woodland directly opposite. Turn left on the farm track and follow this for 350m, soon leaving the Ivanhoe Way and passing through a metal gate, to reach a narrow metalled road with two semi-detached cottages on your right.

Turn left here and follow the road for 100m. Look out for a partly-concealed stile in a very tall hedge on your right. Cross this into the field and walk eastwards, following waymarking signs for 500m with the hedge on your right. Cross a ditch by a waymarked stile and small footbridge on the right and proceed for a further 250m with the hedge now on your left. Approaching the end of the field a finger post directs you across the neck of the field to a stile on to a metalled farm track. Cross this to a stile in the hedge directly opposite. Walk at the side of the field with the hedge on your left for 250m to a hedge at the bottom end. Bear right here and follow a small stream, almost hidden by undergrowth in summer, for 150m, on your left.

Look out for a wide concrete bridge on your left in the corner of the field and use this to cross the stream. Follow a somewhat overgrown path between high hedges towards the village of Newton Burgoland

23

(200m). Pass through a gap in a metal fence by a house and carry on walking straight ahead along Francis Lane for a further 200m to the village main street.

Our walk turns right at the T-junction on the main street, but a diversion to your left takes you, within 75m, to Leicestershire's oldest pub, The Belper Arms, which dates from AD1290.

Resuming the walk, follow the main street for 75m (from T-junction) and then turn right, due south, into The Pinfold. Keep going straight down the lane, ignoring a lane off to your right. After leaving the houses behind, look out for a stile on your right, at a point where the metalled road turns sharply left (300m from main street). Cross the stile on to a gravelled farm track.

After 300m, the track bears right to Field Farm. At this point, cross a stile into a paddock where you should bear slightly right. Cross a double stile and continue southwards through the fields, following good waymarking, for a further 750m, with the hedge at first on your left and then on your right. After crossing a stile go straight across the field to cross another stile beside a metal gate (right of a large ash tree).

Turn left on to a narrow metalled road and follow this for 150m to the T-junction with Heather Road. Turn right towards Shackerstone for 30m and then gain access to the canal towpath by a stile to the right hand side of the canal bridge. Turn left on the towpath and follow this for 300m to the next canal bridge. Leave the towpath at this point. The drive to Shackerstone station is directly opposite (Leicestershire Round long distance footpath sign to point you in the right direction).

Shackerstone station is the northern terminus of the privately-run Battlefield Line which runs along along part of the former route of the old Hinckley-Ashby de la Zouch railway. Just before you reach the station, you cross the River Sence which itself is crossed by the Ashby Canal via an aqueduct. The station and the surrounding marshalling yard are redolent of the vanished age of steam railways. The distinctive architectural style of the old Midland Railway is preserved in the station buildings, the stationmaster's house and the signal box. There is an appetising tea-room in one half of the booking hall and a small but interesting museum in the other.

From the station, follow the gravelled track back, with the canal on your left, for 150m until you reach the metalled lane. Turn left here and cross the canal towards Shackerstone village. Turn left again 75m from the canal. The Rising Sun pub is on your left and is a further agreeable place for refreshments, including food.

Immediately by the pub, turn right and follow Church Walk past Shackerstone's parish church. At the end of Church Walk (200m) turn

Shackerstone station

right onto the highway and follow this for 200m, passing Station Road, until you reach the canal bridge. Cross this and turn immediately left on to the towpath. With the canal on your left, you start the return leg to Snarestone which is 5km to the west/northwest of Shackerstone.

The towpath is in good condition throughout and passes through secluded, well-wooded areas where you will have a chance to see herons and other aquatic wildlife. Look out also for a badger sett at one point.

Close to Snarestone, at canal bridge 59, you will pass a pair of cottages where one of the authors spent a part of his childhood during the Second World War as a refugee from bomb-harassed Birmingham. He knows this section of the canal particularly well as he was walked along it four times a day to and from the village school! Apart from the disappearance of the cottages' outside privvies and the railway bridge across the canal, he assures his co-author that the scene is much as he remembered it. Not a bad recommendation for the walk in a way!

Leave the towpath just before the canal enters a tunnel and emerge on to the car park of the Globe public house for further refreshments before proceeding homewards.

7

The Waterways of
Birmingham West

by John Newson

Starting from Birmingham's prestigious International Convention Centre in the heart of the city this circular walk covers a surprisingly green route via canal towpaths, nature reserves and leafy suburbia.

Distance: 7 miles (11 km).
Maps: Landranger 139; Pathfinder 934; Birmingham A to Z, pages 72,73,88 and 89.
Car Parking: Cambridge Street car park (fee paying).
Public Transport: Buses: all services using Broad Street; Train: Start point is approximately half a mile from Birmingham New Street station.
Start/Finish: International Convention Centre, Broad Street, Birmingham (GR062867) or directly from Broad Street. In this case go down the steps to the left of 'Edwards' (formerly The Crown) and walk forward along the canal to reach the rear entrance to the Convention Centre.
Refreshments: Convention Centre and surrounding area; Gas Street basin (end of walk); pubs: Green Man and The Plough, Harborne.

! On this walk it is necessary to ford Chad Brook which usually has a very low level of water but could be difficult after periods of heavy or prolonged rain.

THE BROAD STREET area of Birmingham has recently been revived after many years of neglect and decay with the building of the International Convention Centre and other new leisure developments that are complemented by the attractive canal network in the area.

From the ICC (rear entrance) immediately cross the canal by the bridge, go down the steps and turn left to walk with the canal on the right. Shortly go left over a bridge opposite the National Indoor Arena (in the direction of Wolverhampton on the signpost). Soon pass under Sheepcote Street bridge and then under St Vincent Street bridge. At the third bridge (Monument Road) leave the canal by the slope to the left and emerge on Ladywood Middleway. Cross the dual carriageway, go left for a few yards and then diagonally right across grassland from the junction of the 'Middleway' and Icknield Square. We are now in Ladywood. Emerge from the grassed area in Freeth Street, turn left and soon turn right into Icknield Port Road, and almost immediately left into Osler Street.

When Reservoir Road is reached turn right (noting the tower of Perrott's Folly beyond the Mount Pleasant Club) to enter the grounds of Edgbaston Reservoir. After passing the Tower Ballroom on the right go right to follow an asphalt path right of the reservoir and then bear left to walk along the dam for a quarter of a mile.

The Edgbaston Reservoir, sometimes known as the Rotton Park Reservoir, was built in 1825 on the site of the Roach Pool. It covers 60

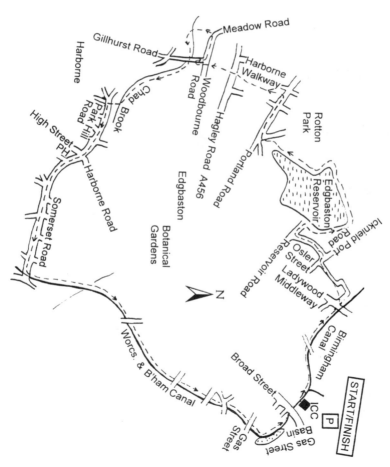

acres and its function was a canal feeder when it was built by Thomas Telford, although leisure use and bird life are its main features now.

Just past the Midland Sailing Club turn left and still walking with the water on the left follow this path for three-quarters of a mile. We are now in Rotton Park – this part of the city takes its name from the medieval hunting park that was enclosed by the Lords of Birmingham and reserved for sport. It was at one time owned by the Rotton family. There are views of the City Centre to the left and a view of St Augustine's Church, Edgbaston, above the trees to the right. Cross a stream feeding the reservoir and then, reaching a second stream, going right to leave the reservoir, passing a bungalow on the right.

From the exit turn left into Rotton Park Road and soon, at the crossroads, turn right into Portland Road: After a quarter of a mile (and 50 yards after crossing Gillott Road) turn left along the disused railway line which has been made into the Harborne Line Walkway. We are now in Edgbaston.

At the first bridge pass under Hagley Road and, after passing under a second bridge, continue forward for 50 yards, then take the path on the right up to the road. Here leave the Walkway and turn right along Gillhurst Road, then left along Woodbourne Road. At the junction of Meadow Road turn left into Chad Brook Walkway.

Chad Brook Walkway is a quiet little piece of unexpected countryside hidden away in Chad Valley. It is bisected by Chad Brook which forms the boundary between Edgbaston and Harborne.

After approximately 50 yards bear left of leisure gardens on a path that (ignoring branches left and right) descends straight ahead to cross Chad Brook (no bridge). Then continue on the same heading along a narrow hedged path for approximately 30 yards and turn first left at a junction of paths. Ignore a branch left and soon reach a pool; go left of it and cross a bridge over the brook and continue left for about 50 yards to go sharp right up a sloping path with fencing on the left to emerge on Gillhurst Road. Cross the road, turn left and rejoin the Walkway on the right.

Turn right along the Walkway which passes through a remarkably wild area which has recently been designated as a nature reserve. Stay on the main track, ignoring side paths, and after half a mile, just before reaching a bridge, turn left off the Walkway and descend into Park Hill Road (adjacent to the bridge). We are now in Harborne.

Turn left along Park Hill Road and shortly, at the junction on North Road bear right across a small sloping recreation ground into Nursery Road and turn right. Soon, at the traffic lights at the Green Man Inn (The Plough is on the right), go straight on along Metchley Lane and shortly take the first left into Somerset Road, passing the Blue Coat School, founded in 1722, on the left. Here we re-enter Edgbaston.

Walk for approximately half a mile along Somerset Road, passing Nuffield Hospital and Queens College on the right and, after crossing Farquhar Road, at the bridge take the steps down to the Birmingham & Worcester Canal. Here turn left to follow the canal for almost two miles back to Birmingham City Centre.

In Edgbaston, well known for its profusion of beautiful trees, the canal follows a green and pleasant route giving the towpath walk a semi-rural feel. Fortunately, industrial developments have always been successfully resisted on this part of the canal by the landowners – the Calthorpe family. From the bridge at The Vale looking to the left beyond the school playing fields there is a view of Birmingham Botanical Gardens which opened in 1832 and were designed by J. C. Loudon, a garden planner and horticultural journalist. It covers 15 acres and its gardens and glasshouses contain a wide variety of plants from all over the world.

Soon we pass through the Edgbaston Tunnel, 105 yards long, and later, after passing Five Ways Station on the left, the canal becomes less scenic as it approaches the City Centre, but Gas Street Basin is soon reached – an interesting and historic area with many opportunities for refreshment. Go under Broad Street and cross the canal bridge to reach the point from which you started.

Canal bridge at The Vale

29

8

Harborne to Hamstead

by Fred Willits

A 'green' walk across Birmingham from south to north, commencing at Chad Brook, going round the Edgbaston Reservoir, then following the Birmingham Canal and, after walking along the River Tame, ending at the Sandwell Valley Nature Reserve (R.S.P.B.) with good opportunities for bird watching.

Distance: (A) 10½ miles (17 km), or (B) 4 miles (6.5 km)
Maps: Landranger 139; Pathfinder 934, 913; Birmingham A-Z
Car Parking: Public transport is more suitable for this linear walk. There is a car park at the end of the walk at the Nature Reserve.
Start: Meadow Road on south side of Hagley Road (A456). GR027858.
Finish: A). Hamstead Road GR039932. A-Z 46 D4 *or* Hamstead railway station. GR050925, A-Z 47 E5.
B)Rabone Lane/Soho Way. GR032885, A-Z 72 B1.
Public Transport: Start: Travel West Midlands 9, 109, 126, 136, 137, 139, 140 to Meadow Road.
Finish: A). Travel West Midlands 16 or train to City Centre; Travel West Midlands 406 to West Bromwich or Scott Arms at Great Barr.
B) Midland Red 440 via Bearwood and Outer Circle to King's Head at Hagley Road, close to start of walk.
Refreshments: The Old Smithy on the corner of Winson Green Road and Norman Street; The London Works Tavern – see text – and other pubs at Rabone Lane, Soho Way and Soho Street intersection, The Royal Oak, Holyhead Road, The Jester, Hamstead Road, Hilltop Golf Club House café.

! The longer route passes through Handsworth Cemetery, the gates of which are closed at 4 p.m. on weekdays, extended to 5 p.m. at weekends and public holidays (except winter months). Make sure that you time your walk so that you are not locked out.

WALK south down Meadow Road. At the bottom of the road turn right into a drive on the corner; then immediately turn sharp left and left again to gain access to the Chad Brook Walkway. Bear right until you reach a footbridge. Cross the bridge and then turn left, crossing over another footbridge and continue along this path. At the crossroads of paths turn right and right again at the next crossroads to walk with a pool on the left. Cross a footbridge and then pass a bridge

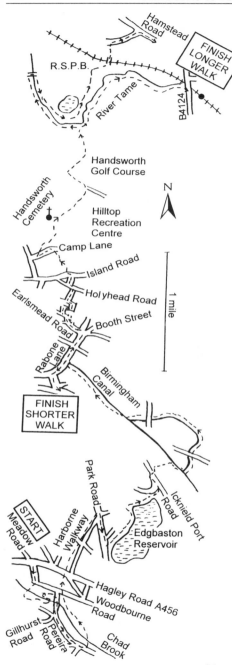

on the left. At the next path junction turn right and follow the path up a small incline to reach a path by a fence. Turn right and follow this path to reach Gillhurst Road. On entering Gillhurst Road cross the road and turn right. Walk to the crossroads and there turn left into Pereira Road. Walk down this road and at the junction with Margaret Grove turn left and at, the next junction, again turn left. Walk along Park Hill Road, passing under the old railway bridge. Immediately after the bridge turn sharp left to gain the now disused Harborne Railway line. Turn right.

The railway line was a legend in its lifetime (1874-1963), although it ceased to carry passengers in 1934. It was known as the Harborne 'Express', the journey taking 22 minutes from New Street to Harborne, returning in 18 minutes. It has been suggested that the speed was such that passengers could pick flowers along the way!

Follow the walkway for about 400 yards until a large chestnut tree, on the other side of a fence on the right is reached, and where the fence ends. Here the path divides. Follow the mesh fence on the left to descend to the Chad Brook and Harborne Nature Reserve. Continue to walk beside the brook, rejoining the main path immediately before a bridge. Pass under the bridge (Woodbourne Road) and two further bridges (Hagley Road, and Portland Road). At the fourth bridge (Rotton Park Road) take the exit from the walkway on the left just before the bridge to enter Rotton Park Road. Cross the road and turn right. Walk along Rotton Park Road, crossing Gillott Road, to gain the entrance to Edgbaston Reservoir, shortly after passing Selwyn Road.

Edgbaston Reservoir was a natural lake which was extended to become a reservoir in relation to the development of the canal system. It is linked with the Icknield canal loop which we meet later. Across the reservoir note Perrott's Folly built by a local landowner in 1758. Subsequently it was the home of the Observatory connected with the Birmingham and Midland Institute.

Walk along the left side of the reservoir passing a shelter, a picnic site and the Midland Sailing Club. Leave the reservoir shortly after passing toilets on the left and before the dam, to enter Icknield Port Road. Turn left and cross the road at the pedestrian crossing. Continue along the road until a pedestrian footway is reached, just after passing Barford School. Turn right and follow the walkway across Barford Road to reach Coplow Street, at its junction with Northbrook Street. Turn right at the junction and then descend steps on the left to reach the Birmingham Canal.

The observant rambler may have noticed the old Harborne railway line

Edgbaston Reservoir

emerging from a tunnel shortly after the start of the walkway from Icknield Port Road to Coplow Street. On reaching the canal the remains of the bridge which carried the railway across the canal to join the main rail track to New Street Station can be seen. From the bridge over the Soho loop a good view of the entrance to the Icknield Port loop can be seen.

Turn right and walk along the canal to the bridge. Cross the canal bridge, and then the bridge over the Soho loop, which is parallel with the railway line; then double back to go under the railway line to gain the towpath on the Soho canal loop. (This is not quite as complicated on the ground as it may seem when reading about it!)

Birmingham is known for its canals. The Birmingham Canal was built by James Brindley and the first section, which connected the Wednesbury collieries to Birmingham, was opened in 1769 and subsequently extended to meet the Staffordshire & Worcestershire Canal north of Wolverhampton. It was a long meandering canal, mostly keeping to contour lines, but with locks taking it over Smethwick Hill. Subsequent improvements were made by John Smeaton and Thomas Telford, and by by-passing several meanders reducing the distance from Birmingham to Wolverhampton by some seven miles. One of the original meanders (which are still in use) is the Soho loop.

At the approach to Western Road bridge look up and note the red wooden partitions in the bridge, inserted to give the Fire Service ready access to a supply of water during WW2.

At Hockley Port cross the arm leading to a small boating community. Continuing along the Soho Loop the towpath passes the City Hospital on the left and All Saints Hospital and Winson Green Prison on the right.

At Asylum bridge a another detour may be made to look at the totem poles and the sculpture on the left bank of the canal; refreshment is available at The Old Smithy.

Continue along the towpath until the Soho loop rejoins the main Birmingham Canal. Turn right and then cross the canal (heading for Wolverhampton). Note the foundations of the old toll house as the canal is crossed.

Another slight detour may be undertaken here by canal/railway enthusiasts. Immediately after crossing the canal climb the grassy embankment to gain the canal feeder running parallel with the canal, which brings water from Edgbaston Reservoir. The extensive railway sidings can be seen on the opposite side of the canal. Continue beside this channel until a track on the right leads back to the towpath; this is opposite a metal bridge on the far bank of the canal.

Walk along the towpath to Rabone Lane bridge where you are now getting a good view of Smethwick industry. Go under the bridge and then take the path on the left up to the road. At the road turn left or, if you are in need of refreshment, turn right and walk to the Rabone Lane, Soho Street, Soho Way intersection. There are a number of pubs in this area, including the London Works Tavern in London Street which had links with the Butler family of Mitchell and Butler fame. The landlady has an interesting collection of newspaper cuttings about the family.

This is the end point for the shorter walk. MRW service 440 will take you from here to Bearwood, close to the start of the walk and from where TWM buses will take you into Birmingham.

To continue the walk from the pub, return to the canal bridge at Rabone Lane.

Walk along Rabone Lane, which soon becomes Booth Street, passing an industrial scene, with a modern gas holder on the right and old bricked up toilets on the left. Immediately after passing under the railway bridge turn sharp left along Crocketts Road, then go left along Earlsmead Road, left again along Junction Road and right along Clarence Road. Take the second left along Raglan Road, then first right along Green Lane passing the children's play area on the right.

Turn left into the busy Holyhead Road to pass the Royal Oak pub and cross at the pelican crossing. Almost opposite is Austin Road, walk up it on the left side to get a view ahead of Barr Beacon. Turn left at the next corner by the holly hedge and cross over the dual carriage way (Island Road, A4040 and Ring Road) shortly to enter Sandwell Recreation Ground on the right. Walk past the children's play area with further views of Barr Beacon through the trees to the right.

As the main path divides bear left to climb up to Camp Lane, crossing a service path to garages on the way. Turn left and walk a short distance to enter Handsworth cemetery on the right. Along this path are a number of Polish graves. At the second crosspaths, at the grave of Jan Slawecki on the right (numbers 37, 42) turn right up a grass path to meet a crossing path with further views. Turn left to reach some steps and go down these.

For toilets, or to visit the cemetery church, turn left to reach the church, taking careful note of the path that you are using. The toilets are at the far end of the church building. Return to the steps and turn left.

Now go forward up another set of steps onto a path lined with poplar trees and follow this to gain the main drive. Turn right and continue to the gates (painted blue at time of writing) and toilets. Turn left to pass a bus shelter (101 route to City) and left along Oxhill Road to an allotment entrance; take the path on the right of the allotment gate to enter the well-named Hilltop Recreation Centre. Almost immediately there is a path division; take the path on the right and walk at the back of the houses, climbing the hill to reach a concrete path.

Bear right skirting the remains of the anti-aircraft battery and ammunition bunkers from WW2. Descend along the concrete path to reach a T-junction; Turn left along a gravel path, swinging right when you reach a playing field to gain a tarmac road. Turn right to pass Hilltop Golf Club house on the right. (The public may use the café and toilets). Continue along this road passing another building on the right; at a signpost on the left to Park Farm turn left on to a gravel path.

Walk along this path between Handsworth (private) golf course on the right and the municipal course on the left to reach the River Tame after crossing a footbridge.

Here you can, if you wish, shorten your walk by about half a mile although this will exclude the Sandwell Valley Nature Reserve. To do this now continue reading from ✱ below.

Continuing with the main walk turn left and walk about 600 yards along the river bank to reach the bridge at Old Forge Mill. Cross the river here and turn right to walk back along the Tame, passing the lake of Sandwell Valley Nature Reserve on the left. The reserve was opened by the R.S.P.B. in 1985 and has three birdwatching hides. Some 170 bird species have been seen here and the grassland attracts many species of butterfly.

As the path swings away from the river take the path on the left to ascend a meandering route to the R.S.P.B. Visitor Centre that you can see ahead. From here you have good views of the lake with direction posts pointing you to the bird hides.

On leaving the Visitor Centre walk along the tarmac driveway, cross the railway to turn right along a road, then right again at the crossroads by Hamstead School into Hamstead Road. From here buses will return you to the city centre. 'The Jester' pub is a short way along on the right.

✱ To shorten the walk turn right along the bank of the River Tame. Note the R.S.P.B. buildings on the other side of the river. Stay on the raised bank, keeping a wary eye for stray golf balls until the path splits. Take the lower path on the left, closer to the river. Continue beside the river until a three-arched bridge is reached. Pass under it and immediately turn right to reach the top of the bridge and continue across it to reach the Old Walsall Road and buses and train to the city centre.

9
Along the Rea Valley
by Edna Irwin

A linear walk, which can be extended with a loop from King's Norton Green to Wychall Reservoir and Hawksley Brook. returning to The Green by the Worcester & Birmingham Canal. It features several items of urban and historical interest in South Birmingham.

Distance: 1) Pebble Mill to Kings Norton – 5 miles (8 km); 2) With loop – 9 miles (14.5 km).
Maps: Landranger 139; Pathfinder 934/954; Birmingham A-Z.
Car Parking: Nature Centre at Pebble Mill, Pershore Rd. (A441) GR 062836; Midlands Art Centre (MAC) at Cannon Hill Park, Edgbaston Road. (B2417) GR 068841.
Public Transport: Buses: *Start*: Travel West Midlands 45, 47, to Pebble Mill; or No.1 from City Centre to Acocks Green passes Cannon Hill Park; *Finish*: Travel West Midlands 45 back to Pebble Mill (or 47 to City Centre; or 11 or 35 according to where one leaves the route.).
Start/Finish: Start at Nature Centre on Pershore Road, opposite Pebble Mill (GR063836) A-Z 89 3G; Finish at 1) Kings Norton Green (GR 049789) A-Z 105 5E; 2) King's Norton Green.
Refreshments: Café at MAC; Pubs: The Lifford Curve, Fordhouse Lane; Navigation Inn, Wharf Road, King's Norton; The Bulls Head, Kings Norton Green; The Camp, Camp Lane.

ALTHOUGH not a majestic river, the River Rea has played an important part in the development of Birmingham over the centuries and it seems a pity that so few residents of the city are aware of the Rea Valley. The river rises in the Waseley Hills and flows through Deritend to join the River Tame. (See Harborne to Hamstead walk, number 8). In 1988 a Rea Valley Conservation Group was formed, with the encouragement of Birmingham City Council, with the aim of protecting the environment and the wildlife along the banks of the river.

This walk follows the river up-stream and the results of the co-operation of the Group and the Council's Leisure and Community Services Department greatly enhance the scene, so that at times one can overlook the fact that one is so close to major roads and the cross-city railway line. Sadly, in some areas litter tends to undermine their efforts.

The walk starts at Pebble Mill, where there was once a thriving rolling mill, but the area is better known to-day for the BBC Television Centre, which is situated in Pebble Mill Road on the opposite side of the Pershore Road to the Nature Centre.

Facing the entrance to the Nature Centre take the path immediately to the left of the building. Follow it to the Scout War Memorial. Turn left and walk beside the River Rea. After passing a bridge on the right descend the steps on the right to the river. Walk left a short distance down the river and immediately after passing another bridge, ascend the steps on the left. Turn right at the top of the steps. Cross the bridge on the right to enter Cannon Hill Park at MAC (*Midlands Arts Centre* – in addition to a cinema, theatre and a bookshop there are toilets and a café.).

From MAC, facing the pool turn left and walk beside the pool, passing the boating kiosk. Just before the bridge turn left to view the model of the Elan Valley (the source of Birmingham's water supply). Continue along this path and cross a footbridge to re-join the main path. Turn right and walk back towards the bridge.

Turn left immediately before the bridge to fork left and walk away from the pool and then take the next path on the right to reach the Boer War Memorial. At the memorial turn left and walk away from it to reach the main drive through the park from the entrance gate. Turn right and continue along this drive, passing The Garden Tea-room, Cannon Hill Park 'station' and 'Ye Olde Golden Lion' (This former fifteenth century pub was moved from its original site in Deritend). Take the first track on the left after passing the 'pub' and continue to a T-junction.

Here turn right, then left at the next T-junction. Walk a short distance to the top of the incline and turn right through trees to enter the RSPB Centenary Nature Reserve. Turn right, with trees on your right, and walk about 100 yards to a gate on the right. Leave the reserve by the gate to re-enter the park. At the T-junction turn left and then almost immediately take a path on the left. Follow the path along the fence for about a third of a mile skirting the allotments on the left, and a play area on the right, until a tarmac path is reached. This path skirts a sports pitch.

Turn left and walk through the metal traffic calming barriers, keeping the sports pitch on the right. At the T junction walk across the road and take a path almost exactly opposite, and left of a brick British Gas building, which veers to the right, to enter Holder's Wood. Continue along this track through the wood keeping parallel with the rear garden fencing, passing ponds, to emerge from the wood and enter a small field. Keeping the same bearing cross this field to a gap in the hedge and another field to reach the tarmac path at the back of Moor Green Medical Centre.

Turn left along this path and then, just before a gate, go diagonally right along a path to reach Moor Green Lane. (Bus route 69 Kings Heath to Weoley Castle).

Turn right and walk to the bridge over the River Rea. Cross the road and take the way-marked Rea Valley cycle/pedestrian route to the left of the bridge. Follow this until Cartland Road (named after Barbara's family) is reached. Cross the road and continue along the Rea valley route, with the river on the right – a rather industrial area. (Note the footbridge opposite Philip Harris but do not take it.) Cross the road bridge on the right at Selco, on the Stirchley trading estate and then turn left to continue beside the river until Fordhouse Lane is reached (A4040; 11 Outer Circle bus route.)

Cross the road with care, and turn left to take a track immediately on the right and cross to a lamppost at the back of a row of houses. Walk along the flagged path behind the houses, turning left at the end into Harvest Close. (The river flows into a culvert at this point.) Walk through the Close (ignoring a cul-de-sac left) to reach a T-junction. (The Worthings).

Turn right and walk under the railway bridge (used as an air raid shelter in WW2) along The Pathway (A-Z 105 2G). Continue to Allens Croft Road, with Pineapple School facing. Turn right and walk along Allens Croft Road, passing the neighbourhood office and King's Heath Elim church, to its continuation into Brandwood Park Road. This rather sharp corner is marked with a chevron at which there is a forked track on the right. Take the left one to rejoin the river as it emerges from the culvert.

Follow this path by the river, crossing the footbridge. Continue until a flight of steps is noticed on the left. Climb the steps to reach Lifford Reservoir. Walk along the right side of the reservoir, passing the psychedelic boat-house on the right to turn right into Tunnel Lane. Walk down the lane, passing Lifford Hall (now the base for a firm of certified accountants, but once the home of Viscount Lifford of Donegal; sadly it is overshadowed now by the unsightly chimney of the chemical firm Rhone-Poulenc).

On reaching Lifford Lane turn left, noting the Lifford lions' heads on the bridge. Cross the road when the footpath ends (for safety) and walk past the Lakeside Centre, presumably named after the nearby mill pond.

Just before the canal bridge cross the road again and take the path down to the Stratford-upon-Avon Canal. Turn right, walking under the bridge. (Note the guillotine gates or doors of the stop lock, now always open, but originally placed to prevent the loss of water from the Worcester to the Birmingham canal). Continue along the towpath and across the bridge over the Birmingham & Worcester Canal. From the bridge note the helicopter pad and walkway to the Lakeside Centre.

After crossing the canal turn left (Note the old house at the junction of the Stratford and Birmingham & Worcester canals with its interesting plaque about the Birmingham & Worcester Canal, and the signposts indicating the miles and locks to Warwick and Worcester.) Facing the Junction House take a path to the right of it, leading to a recreation ground; this involves crossing a new bridge and up-graded path. At the end of the path beside pre-fab green huts, turn left, crossing a small stream close to the huts, and walk uphill towards buildings..

Past the last tree on the left, and at the back of the buildings, is an alleyway leading to Pershore Road South. On reaching Pershoré Road

South turn left and walk towards King's Norton Green, passing Kings Norton Primary School and the Navigation Inn on the left. Kings Norton Green is on the right-hand side of Pershore Road South at the roundabout. (It is safest to cross the road at the pelican crossing). Refreshments are available here before continuing with the loop, and buses are available back to the start of the walk at Pebble Mill.

Whatever decision is made it is worth while spending a little time exploring the Green – the Saracen's Head , St Nicholas' church and the Old Grammar School, at the back of the church, linked with John Baskerville.

To continue the longer walk leave The Green by Back Road, to the right of the church, or through the churchyard, keeping to the right of the church and walking towards the Old Grammar School, to regain Pershore Road South. Turn left – that is towards the City Centre. After a short distance turn left into King's Norton Park and immediately turn right to walk towards a footbridge. Turn left before the footbridge and walk, with the stream on the right, to join a path coming in on the left. Continue along this path.

At a children's play area and flowerbeds turn right to cross a footbridge. Immediately turn left and walk beside the stream, with tennis court on the right. On reaching the disused toilets and changing rooms, pass to the right of the building and turn right to reach Westhill Road. Cross the road and over the bridge, then past two houses to take a riverside path on the left. Follow this path along the River Rea, keeping parallel to the fencing of factory sites on the right. (At the time of writing a number of factory buildings were being demolished here and some redevelopment of the area seems likely.)

Arriving at a tarmac drive at a former factory gate turn left and cross the bridge. Walk along the drive for about 75 yards and then take a kissing gate on the right to reach Wychall Reservoir. Walk along with the river on the left and the reservoir, followed by a stream, on the right. (It is interesting to see how much developments related to the canals add to our enjoyment to-day.) Cross the footbridge to reach Pope's Lane.

Turn left and walk past St Thomas Aquinas School to a T-junction (where Wychall Lane and Wychall Road meet). Cross the road to take the footpath facing Pope's Lane. There is a gentle ascent, past Tower blocks to Vardon Way. Cross Vardon Way, but look back and note the view of Frankley Beeches – a clump of trees on a hilltop (829 ft) near Northfield, given to the National Trust in memory of the late Richard and George Cadbury, 'to be an open space for ever'. Unfortunately, at the time of writing, the plaque with this information had been removed. About face and continue along the path to reach Rednal Road. (It should by now be apparent that the route is following part of the circumference of a circle with St Nicholas' church at its centre).

Cross Rednal Road, turn right and after 50 yards enter an alleyway on the left. Follow this out into Grange Farm Drive (passing Headley Croft on the right) and re-enter an alleyway to arrive at Redditch Road. Cross the dual carriageway and turn left to walk to Branch Road on the right. Take this road to a 'mound'. Cross it diagonally and over Longdales Road to enter Lime Walk, just to the left of a bus stop, passing Old Lime Gardens on the right. This was the main drive to Hawksley Hall, which was demolished and the land developed for housing between the wars. Cross over the crossing path (Eckington Walk) and continue through a wooded area to emerge on Shannon Road (TWM 35 route, MRW 83).

Cross the road and walk down the grassy slope facing, beside a wooden fence on the right (near a bus stop). At the bottom turn right and immediately cross the bridge on the left and follow Hawksley Brook (on your left), passing West Mill Croft and Glenroyd. Soon turn left and continue to follow the brook, passing Hawkesley School to gain Bargehorse Walk, so-called as it was the path for the horses as the barges were legged through the Wasthill Tunnel. Turn left into Bargehorse Walk to skirt the school and regain Shannon Road. Cross it and continue along Bargehorse Walk, over a crossing path, until a junction of paths is reached – a mini 'Fiveways'. Here go straight over and take a dirt track to the right of a lamp post.

Follow this path along a metal fence on the right until an air vent to the canal tunnel some thirty feet below appears on the left. Continue along the path as it veers left and ascends steeply, then walking parallel with the road (over to your left) until it joins a flagged path. Turn right and skirt the back of King's Norton High School (until recently Primrose Hill secondary school, and not to be confused with Primrose Hill J&I school which is on the left). Go through two underpasses and continue straight ahead over crossing path. Pass Tunnel Cottage and immediately descend steps on the right to the Birmingham & Worcester Canal. Glance back on the towpath to note the canal emerging from Wasthill Tunnel.

Turn left and walk beside the canal, passing under a services bridge and the newly constructed bridge at Masshouse Lane. At the next bridge (no.71) go under the bridge and immediately turn left to go up to Wharf Road. Turn right and follow the road past the Navigation Inn to finish the walk at Pershore Road South at King's Norton Green.

The energetic might consider continuing to walk along the canal to Selly Oak on the Bristol Road (2½ miles) – 61, 62 and 63 bus routes to City Centre; or even to Gas Street Basin, near the International Convention Centre in Broad Street (5¼ miles).

10
Harvington Hall and Blakedown

by Carol and David Carter

This circular walk is easy going and very near Birmingham in beautiful countryside, starting at the Roman Catholic stronghold of Harvington Hall with its association with the Gunpowder Plot, including four hiding places which were priest holes.

> **Distance:** 9 miles (14.5 km).
> **Maps:** Landranger 139; Pathfinder 953.
> **Car Parking:** Harvington Hall, turning left from Birmingham off the A450 opposite The Dog public house.
> **Public Transport:** Bus Midland Red West 192; alight at The Old House at Home in Blakedown. Start reading from ✱ on page 45.
> **Start/Finish:** Harvington Hall (GR879754) or Blakedown (GR880784).
> **Refreshments:** Pubs in Blakedown and Harvington. During season meals and snacks at Harvington Hall.

START from Harvington Hall with its large water filled moat supporting a variety of waterfowl. From the car park go back along the route by which you arrived to the bend in the lane where there is a public footpath sign on the right (direction N.E), opposite an old quarry. Proceed at first along a farm-cart track with the hedge on the right and after this turns right continue straight ahead on a footpath, still with the hedge on the right. Go in the same direction through a gap in a hedge which is at right angles to the path. A short distance later, still going N.E., carry on with the now rudimentary hedge on the left.

Where a fence with trees comes in from the left turn left through a narrow gap in the hedge and immediately right over a waymarked stile and carry on forward with the hedge on the right. After 75 yds, at the next corner turn left with the hedge still on the right for 50 yds to the next corner where you turn right over two stiles and proceed for 50 yds along a narrow path. At its end turn left over a stile and immediately right, still going N.E. to gain a lane over a stile to the right of a gate.

On the lane turn right and after 50 yds by a footpath signpost go left, at first on a drive that soon curves left to a house – you, however, go straight on with fields on the right and a hedge on the left. Cross a stile

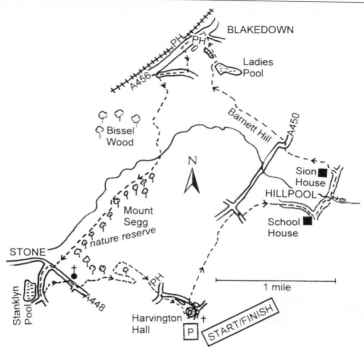

to the right of a gate, then just before the next fence turn left over a stile to the left of a gate. Go forward a few yards by the gate and then turn 45 degrees towards the right, facing almost east. Cross a field to a stile and over this descend to a lane where you turn right. Follow this, ignoring the road left to Hillpool, until you reach 'School House' on the right.

Opposite this turn sharp left over a bar by a signpost and descend by a narrow path, at first with Christmas trees of all sizes on the left, to reach a small gate. Go through this and past a house on the right, following its drive to reach a lane in Hillpool where you turn right to cross a very noisy brook, once used for scythe making.

To see the attractive mill pool go up the drive to The Old Mill and Stable Cottage on the right and then, on reaching the gates to Stable Cottage turn right along a path to a bridge over the stream.

Return to the brook and walk uphill on the lane for about half a mile to pass the entrance to Sion House, then Sion Court and Sion Farm, where you turn left as shown by a signpost and a sign to Sion Farm Fishery. With the farm on your left, ignoring the sign 'STOP NO ENTRY', turn left round the farm and immediately right, making for the green sheds to your left to proceed along a bridlepath and keeping the sheds on the right.

The bridlepath becomes a tarmac lane and reaches the A450. Cross this with great caution (*dangerous bend, fast traffic!*) and proceed uphill past a gate on a bridlepath onto Barnett Hill from where extensive views can be obtained (the Clent hills to the north-east; the Clees to the west, and the Malverns south-south-west). At the end turn right onto a lane which bends to the left after 30 yds and continue on it for 300 yds until you see a public footpath signpost on the right with a stile, which you cross, to walk with the hedge on the right.

At a division of the path take the right-hand fork which leads to the shores of 'Ladies Pool'. There take the left fork and continue with the tranquil water on the right. At a waymark post go right, still round the pool.

Ladies Pool, or Lady Pool as it was originally known, together with Forge Pool to your left, were constructed in the eighteenth century to provide water power for a nearby forge and mills. Lady Pool was considerably enlarged at the time of the Napoleonic Wars by French prisoners who were being held at Kidderminster, and it was they who constructed the dam along which you walk.

On emerging from the surrounding wood onto fields take the left path following the wood on the left, continuing through a gap in the hedge at right angles. There are glimpses of Forge Pool through the trees

Ladies Pool

on the left. On reaching a lane by houses turn right and emerge onto the busy A456 in Blakedown by the side of the Old House at Home pub. Turn left along this road.

✳ *Start here if you are using public transport.*

Walk south-west along the A456 for 200 yds to pass The Swan pub on the right. 120 yds further on, with glimpses of Swan Pool on the left, turn left along a signed bridleway (sign of Halfshire Lane at right angles) and bear right at the end of it, between houses, to go uphill on a narrow path. This joins a lane at the top where you turn right. Where the lane swings right, just before reaching the main road, turn left round a white house onto a bridlepath. Continue on it, veering slightly right where a fence on the left ends, to reach Deansford Lane, opposite Bissel Wood.

Turn left along the lane and after about 200 yds, just before a farm on the left, turn right by a bridlepath signpost, going straight on, not through the gate on the right. After 230 yds the bridlepath veers left, crosses one stream and quickly follows another one on your left, which you soon cross and immediately turn right with the stream now on the right. Proceed along a woodland path through a Nature Reserve with Mount Segg on the left. Reaching a stile meet a hairpin bend, and take the lower fork along a lane. Ignoring turns off go straight on to reach the A448. Turn right and then first left along Stanklyn Lane, passing Stanklyn Pool largely hidden by woodland on the right. When you reach a turning to the right, turn left by a public footpath sign and go up to a stile to the right of a gate. Cross this and turn left to reach another stile slightly to the right of a large oak tree and make for the spire of St Mary's Church, Stone, going over another stile onto the A448.

Cross the road and turn right to pass the church, noting the fine wooden gates into the churchyard, and then, just beyond Butts Lane to the right, turn left over a waymarked stile to the left of a gate. You now follow the left-hand zigzag edge of a large field, also passing Stone House Cottage Garden Nurseries with its attractive buildings, until you reach the final tip of a wood on your left. (*This path has been officially diverted and so does not now follow the route shown in Ordnance Survey maps.*) Here turn left over a stile and go steeply downhill to cross a stream and then up again. At the top climb over a stile on the right and turn left (N.E.) along a fence and rudimentary hedge on your left. After 150 yds look out for the waymark post on the left and turn right (S.E.) on a right of way across a large field (the path is not very obvious), making for an apex of hedges.

Fork right here (waymarked) and with the hedge on your left go over a stile to the left of a gate. Keep leftish on the upper plateau, not following a cart track going downhill on the right. Keep another fence on your left until you reach and cross a stile by the side of The Dog.

Cross the A450 *very carefully*, turn right for about 50 yards, then take the drive on the left between Forge Cottage on the left and a garden on the right. Where the drive swings right go ahead on a path with a hedge on the left. Cross a stile and continue forward with a fence on the right passing some attractive pools to reach the moat of Harvington Hall. A path off to the left will give you good views of the moat and of the rear of the Hall. Then continue back to the car park.

Now continue reading from the start of this chapter if you started from Blakedown.

The moated Harvington Hall

11

Secret Pools and Quiet Streams

by Clive Hough

This very satisfying full day's walk explores some of the small streams and discovers secret out-of-the-way pools in the lovely countryside of North Worcestershire. The walk also takes in woodlands, small ridges with glorious views, and the historic villages of Chaddesley Corbett and Harvington with its Tudor hall. There's good public transport, seven days a week, at the start and finish of the walk, so why not leave the car at home?

> **Distance:** 13 miles (21 km), 8½ miles (13.5 km) or 4½ miles (7 km).
> **Maps:** Landranger 138/139; Pathfinder 953.
> **Public Transport:** *Out*: Travel West Midlands 62, Birmingham City Centre to Rednal. From the terminus walk forward about 100 yards to the Visitor Centre; *Return*: Midland Red West 192/3 or Train, Kidderminster to Birmingham
> **Start:** Rednal Visitor Centre (GR000760)
> **Finish:** Kidderminster (GR832763)
> **Refreshments:** Inns and tea rooms in Rednal and Chaddesley Corbett; Inns at Wildmoor, Bournheath,and Harvington
> **Shorter versions:** The walk can be terminated (A) after 4½ miles at Fairfield (MRW 318/319, Bromsgrove/Stourbridge) or (B) after 8½ miles at Chaddesley Corbett (MRW 133/134/136, Kidderminster/Bromsgrove).

THE walk starts at the Visitor Centre, Rednal, where snacks and refreshments are available. It contains an interesting display of information and photographs of Birmingham's old trams. Cross the road using the nearby pelican crossing and turn left on the far side so that you are walking south, downhill. Just before the traffic island bear right with the path to join the B4096 (Rose Hill). As the main road bends left uphill walk up the drive of the golf course on your right, then bear left to pass in front of the Old Rose and Crown Hotel. Behind the hotel there is an attractive series of pools fed by a stream coming down off Beacon Hill.

Take the path along the right-hand side of the first lake. At the far end of this ignore the path over the footbridge on your left and keep ahead with the stream on your left.

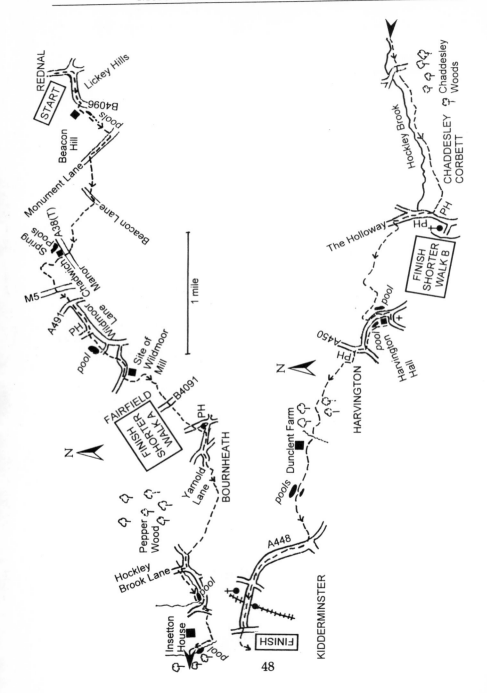

At the next junction of paths cross the stream and bear half right: on your left is a lovely area of sloping grass with picnic tables, an ideal place to linger and enjoy the attractive surroundings.

The stream should now be on your right. Follow the path, climbing gently, ignoring footbridges on your right and paths off. The path bends left, then very soon sharp right, before trees, to climb more steeply.

Almost at the top of the hill the path splits: take the left fork to reach Monument Lane. Cross the lane and turn right along this for about 200 yards. Just after the last house on the left take the fieldpath signed 'Beacon Lane and Bristol Road'. The path goes diagonally across the field, crossing a drive by stiles, descending to another stile across the next field, then ascending slightly in the following field to an exit site on Beacon Lane. There are good views south over Bromsgrove to the Malvern, Abberley and Bredon Hills.

Turn left along Beacon Lane for about 100 yards and take the footpath on the right along the drive to Beacon Farm. At the end enter a path into pleasant woodlands, passing a pond on the right. This path descends and swings left, passing a stone memorial seat to Alderman Jack Wood, a man who loved the countryside to the west of Birmingham and who was a former Rambling Correspondent for the *Birmingham Post*.

Going through a gate at the end of the wood s you now walk through the beautiful garden of a National Trust owned house. At the road turn right into a cul-de-sac. A tarmac path at its far end on the left leads to the main road A38(T).

Cross very carefully, via the gap in the barrier in the central reservation, to the other side of the road at the bus shelter. Steps down to a stile and signpost to its left mark our next path. Cross the stile, then glance down right: you will get a good view of Spring Pools behind the eighteenth century Chadwich Manor. Descend sharply to a stile beside a gate onto the drive left of the manor house. Follow the drive out to a lane, then turn right.

When the lane bends right take the farm drive on the left. Continue past the farm buildings on the track and, just before a gate into a field go through a gate on the left. Walk along a path hedged on both sides for about 50 yards until, just before the end of the left-hand hedge, you see an easily missed stile on your left into an enclosed area. Walk down this area of young planted trees, keeping to the fence on your left, to a stile.

Cross over into a field, bearing right to a tunnel under the M5. You are now on the Monarch's Way, a long distance path (610 miles, Worcester to Shoreham) that follows the route taken by Charles II as he was pursued by Cromwell's forces after Charles' defeat at the battle of

Worcester. Immediately after passing through the tunnel-turn left into a field, then bear right, aiming to the left of a group of trees. In the hedge you will find a stile; cross this onto the A491(T).

Cross the busy main road carefully and walk along Wildmoor Lane opposite. After a quarter of a mile you reach a junction with a lane to the right, where a few yards along is the Wildmoor Oak Inn. Enter the pub car park on the left. Cross the stile facing you and bear right to follow the right-hand hedge. In the following field, as you pass the garden of a house on the left, will be found our next water feature, an attractive reed-fringed pool with a small island in its centre.

Keeping the pool on your right, cross an easily missed stile about 20 yards before the end of the field, then continue forward with a fence on your left. Cross a driveway via stiles and very shortly go over another stile into a field. Walk through this and a following field to come out on a lane at a bend. Follow the lane ahead and round the bend to pass a white painted house and the site of the former Wildmoor Mill.

Continue along the lane for about 150 yards and then, at a white footpath sign on the left, cross a stile into a field. Go along the right-hand hedge, cross a stile and bear slightly left across the field, aiming left of large barns, to reach a stile in the opposite hedge. Cross the stile and follow the left-hand hedge to reach and cross a stile onto a farm drive. Turn right to follow the drive, climbing steadily uphill to reach the B4091

For the shorter walk A turn right along the B4091 into Fairfield and buses to Bromsgrove and Stourbridge.

A path is signed along a drive almost opposite. Follow the drive, continuing ahead between hedges where the drive bends right. The path bends right, then left onto a track between a new bungalow on the left and a hedge on the right. Just before a 'Private Property' sign the way is arrowed down an enclosed path to the right, leading through a field to a lane at Bournheath.

Turn left and after a few yards take, on the right, an enclosed path with a hedge on the right and a low wall on the left. The path soon crosses a private drive to skirt the grounds of The Gate public house on your left.

At the lane turn right, uphill, to a junction. Take Yarnold Lane opposite and, after about 250 yards – just before a house on your left, take a signed path on the right, over a stile. Keep the hedge on your right, over several stiles, to gradually descend the hill. There are glorious views south over the Worcestershire countryside.

The path soon bears right across a stile with a hedge now on your left. Bear slightly right to cross the corner of the field diagonally to reach a stile. Go over this and continue forward across the following field, into a dip where you cross a stile and walk up the field with a hedge on your left. At the corner, cross a stile and keep in the same direction, the hedge now being on your right. We are now entering a well-wooded area of Worcestershire: Pepper Wood is visible over to your right.

At the next corner cross the stile, then bear slightly right, aiming left of buildings ahead. Cross another stile, then go across a small field to a stile and out to a lane. Turn left, then take Hockley Brook Lane on the right.

After about 50 yards and after crossing a barely visible brook, turn left over a stile into a field. Keep a hedge and the brook on your left and then, as they swing left, aim towards the barns ahead, crossing a stile on the way. Insetton House can be seen on the hillock ahead. Approaching the farm, walk to the right and go through a pair of gates to pass a lovely pool on your left. Soon moving away from the hedge on your right, exit onto a lane via a gate on a concrete drive.

Turn right on the lane, then left at the junction along Woodcock Lane. After about 50 yards take the signed path over a stile on your right, then follow the right-hand hedge along the field to a corner stile with a wood to your left. This is a particularly lovely section of the walk, gently undulating where one can feel a sense of isolation.

After crossing a stile turn right, then immediately left, to pass a waymarked post on your left. Go ahead, walking towards a wood with a ditch and an orchard on your left. Reaching the wood, a marker post

Approaching Insetton House

indicates the path right. Another attractive pool is soon reached on your left. This makes an excellent picnic spot, quiet and secluded, with the trees forming a backcloth.

About 75 yards after the pool a waymark arrow directs the path left into the trees. Cross a stile and turn immediately sharp left, ignoring a footbridge to your right. The stream is the Hockley Brook, the valley of which we shall follow for the next 1½ miles. Go along the path, which was slightly overgrown on my visit, to a footbridge with Chaddesley Woods, a National Nature Reserve, beyond. Cross the bridge and bear right with the path, passing a notice-board, and over a stile into a field.

Go up the field, with Hockley Brook wriggling its way below you to your right. Cross three stiles in succession aiming, after the first stile, to the right of a house. After the third stile reach a lane. Turn left up the lane for a few yards to a footpath, signed Briar Hill, on your right.

Cross the stile and keep ahead, picking up the wood on your left-hand side. In the corner cross the stile, then follow the path veering left, cutting through a corner of the wood to another stile into an open field. Cross the stile and turn right to follow the right-hand hedge, keeping ahead when the hedge bears right in a dip. Climb slightly to a gap in the facing hedge, go through and bear right across the field to an electricity pylon, crossing the stile behind it.

You will now see a gate ahead: cross the stile to its left onto a gravel drive, then go over the stile opposite. In the far hedge, left of the corner, go through a gap, then continue forward to the next field corner where there is a metal gate. Go through and walk to the stile ahead in the corner, passing a footbridge on your right.

Cross the stile and head across the field, keeping right of the pylon, then cross two stiles over a farm drive. Keep in the same direction over the field to cross another stile near the left corner of the field. Here there is a fine view to Chaddesley Corbett church steeple, backed by the distant Abberley Hills.

The path is now clear across two arable fields: at the far hedge of the second largest field you meet a T-junction of paths. Turn right and follow the path, now a track, by one of two routes into Chaddesley Corbett. For the shorter route cross a stile where the track swings left and go forward to emerge opposite the Swan Inn. But to see more of this charming village continue around a right bend, passing a farm, and into the main street.

For the shorter walk B you can take the MRW 133/134/136 service from here. A few buses leave from the Talbot Inn but for most you will need to turn left to the A448 (Chaddesley Turn).

At the village street turn right and, if you took the longer route, walking past the church on your left and the Talbot Inn, built on a sandstone base, on your right.

At the far end of the village street you cross the Hockley Brook for the last time, then take the next fork left uphill, along The Holloway, cut deep in the sandstone. Almost at the top of the hill take a signed track on your left past a house (Green Acres). Walk along a grassy path to a gate but don't go through; instead go through a concealed hedge gap on your right, adjacent to the gate. The path goes ahead across an arable field, soon picking up a right-hand hedge and becoming a track. Enjoy the views with, to the left, the Abberleys (south-west) and the Malverns (south). Go through a gate and then, about half-way along the field, swap sides of the hedge, over a stile, to continue in the same direction, now with the hedge on the left-hand side.

At the corner of the field go through a gap, turn left along a track and at the next corner go right. Walk past a private drive on your left and after about 200 yards turn left to meet a lane. Go left, following the lane between attractive pools and passing the remains of an ancient oak to reach the Tudor Harvington Hall, surrounded by its moat. If you have the time the house is well worth a visit, among the features of interest being the priests' hiding holes.

Turn into the car park of Harvington Hall and go through a gate to pass the Hall and its moat on your right.

Keep ahead on the track and you will soon pass more pools on your right. Stay on the grassy bank above the attractive pools, with the houses of Harvington to the right. Soon cross a stile to walk with a hedge on your right to the corner of the field, then go forward to the A450 at Harvington.

Turn right and cross the main road carefully to a signposted stile on your left, just before the Dog Inn. Cross the stile and walk forward, initially with a fence on the right, climbing slightly to join a farm track coming in from your left; turn right along it. Cross a stile and keep ahead to where the hedge on your right bends to the right sharply. Here turn left (WNW) to take a path straight across the arable field to a facing hedge. Go through a gap in the hedge, turn right, then after a few yards left to continue following the clear path to a slight dip at the far side of the field. Go left, with the hedge on your right, very soon taking a path on the right to descend into a beautiful wooded valley.

Reaching the edge of the wood the path bears right, briefly following a path, then crosses a stile to join a farm track. Turn right along this, go through a gate and turn left, then after a few yards take another track on the right signed (on the adjacent telegraph post) to Dunclent Farm.

A 'secret pool' near the end of the walk

As you leave the wooded area cross a stream and, before the farm, go left over a stile. Cross (WNW) to the stile in the fence ahead and look left at an attractive pool below. Go left across the next field with a fence on the right and make for a stile ahead. The path now follows a green track, making for pleasant walking as it passes between two more lovely pools, the pool on the right being in a particularly nice setting.

Keep following the track to eventually emerge onto the main Bromsgrove-Kidderminster road (A448) where you turn right and follow it into Kidderminster town centre. The contrast between the quiet paths you have just walked and the busy main road could not be greater; it surprised me!

If you wish to avoid the traffic you could, at this point, take the local bus service (MRW 18) or MRW 133/134 to the railway and bus stations. But check the timetable because it may be quicker to walk. The nearest stop for MRW 18 is about 50 yards along Spennells Valley Road.

Otherwise, as you approach the town centre you pass the railway station on your left where there is a good service of trains to Birmingham. Bus users must continue down the hill, crossing the ring road at the bottom using the subway and into Oxford Street (Town Centre direction). Pass a drinking fountain with a clock and take New Road on your left, then take the third street on your right, Corporation Street; this leads into the bus station. A MRW 192 bus will take you back to Birmingham.

12
Sapey Brook

by Joan Jenkinson and Pat Holmes

This is a circular walk with wide vistas of the beautiful woods and rolling green hills of Worcestershire with the Malverns in view from the higher ridges. The route follows the Sapey Brook (a tributary of the River Teme) for much of the way, then joins the Teme for the latter part of the walk. The ancient settlement of Lower Sapey is included where the gradual restoration of the derelict church and adjoining Sapey Court can provide continuing interest for return visits. Don't forget your camera on this walk!

Distance: 12 miles (19 km).
Maps: Landranger 149; Pathfinder 995/973.
Car Parking: Roadside to the east of the starting point.
Public Transport: Midland Red West 419/420 Worcester/Hereford. Alight at the Wheatsheaf, Sapey Bridge.
Start/Finish: Sapey Bridge, The Wheatsheaf Inn on the A44 (Worcester to Bromyard road) (GR717562).
Refreshments: The Wheatsheaf Inn, Sapey Bridge; Live and Let Live Inn, Meadow Green. Nothing available *en route*

TAKE the minor road past the Wheatsheaf northwards for a short way. This immediately crosses Sapey Brook by the County Bridge (no. 254). After about 30 yards ignore the locked gates on your left but just beyond, and before the unusual building, turn left and left again to pass through a small stone archway which leads into an orchard. Keep to the right in a westerly direction to a waymarked stile.

Over the stile keep the hedge on your right to a stile and a bridge over the brook with its waterfall. Over the next stile turn right and with the hedge on your right take a line across the field which passes the second telegraph pole from the right. This line will bring in view a waymarked gate ahead across a metalled path.

Through this gate go up the hill keeping to the right and following the fence past the woods and past a field to a field gate directly ahead. Turn right here.

Go through the next gate and bearing to the right go downhill to a further gate. After this, keep to the fence on your left and continue downhill a short way to a footbridge over Paradise Brook. Cross it and go through a gate ahead. Follow the track uphill to a road gate.

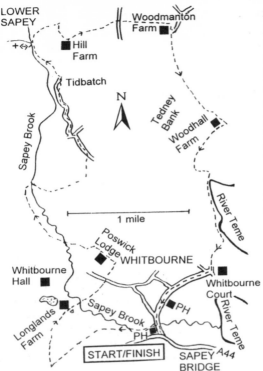

Turn right along the road, then left over a cattle grid and along the farm driveway to cross the stream and walk in front of Longlands Farm. This is a delightful spot to pause and absorb the gracious atmosphere of the fine buildings and the bird-frequented pools.

Continue by following the stream to your right round the curve of the hill, cutting across left to pass by four magnificent wellingtonias (sequoias) to an iron footbridge where we rejoin the Sapey Brook. Note the decorative stone bridge on your right which previously flanked an approach to Whitbourne Hall (now out of view to the left).

Cross the footbridge, turn right and, after negotiating a boggy patch, continue in this north-easterly direction, keeping first a stream, then a fence, and finally a hedge on your right (ignore an enticing footbridge) until directly ahead you come to a hedge-stile which leads to a road.

Cross the road and go over the stile opposite. Keep to the same line and pass between willows to a stile in the corner beyond. Over this, turn left and, keeping the hedge and a pool (half-hidden by the trees) on your left, follow the field edge to a stile in the corner. Cross it, turn left, pass through a gate, then go diagonally right, across the field, towards the farm by Poswick Lodge.

Waymark arrows direct you through the farmyard, through a gate opposite and down to a stile and gate leading to a track. Turn left along this. A short way down, the track bends left but a waymark post points the way to the right.

Go right, over a stile beside an iron gate and into an orchard. An old track, dark beneath the tangled trees, can soon be seen on the left, which would be our way were it not so overgrown and interrupted by barbed

56

wire fencing. Keep by the old track down to the bottom of the field, then go left through the gate there and right, through the gate beyond.

Keeping Sapey Brook *on your left* go up to a low bridge over it and cross. Continue following the brook, *now on your right*, past the white house to a hedged track. Follow the track until, after crossing a field, the brook can be either forded or crossed by a footbridge on your left. *With three miles now completed this may make a peaceful refreshment stop.*

You are now in a field bordered on three sides by woods. With Sapey Brook out of sight in the woods on the left go up this field, keeping to the left of the slope, to a gate on the right at the far end (ignoring a nearby stile on the left) which leads into the woods. Turn right onto the bridlepath and follow it uphill through a gate, a field with a hedge on the left, and a further gate onto a track. Continue to the top of the hill past Primrose Cottage, then pause to admire a delightful oak-sheltered pond, and on through Lee Lay Farm.

Soon the track, now metalled, passes a long wooden-slatted barn of Woodhall Farm and a fine tennis court to join a road. Turn left along this and after a short distance, and having passed a wood-shingled house on the right, take the first minor road left. Keep to this for about half a mile as it turns downhill and sinks deeper to expose head-high tree roots. Past the stables the road bends left and becomes more track-like. Continue past an old black and white building until, just before reaching the buildings at Tidbatch (at a sign 'Tidbatch. Private') the sharp-sighted will spot a bridleway sign on a fence to the right. This directs you right, through a gate.

Here the way is bordered by ornamental trees of rich colours in the autumn. A further gate leads through to the woods where you bear right.

Here we meet the Sapey Brook again deep to our left. The track very soon crosses the brook itself and bears to the left until a path can be seen at the corner of the field on your right which follows the right hand edge of the wood along a field hedge. This footpath may be rather overgrown in full summer.

Follow along the path until, after about 100 yards, there is a gate on your right. Here the path becomes more distinct to the left. Take it and go downhill along a particularly delightful section of the walk and past Waste Common Cottage to rejoin the brook. Further along, a bridge is reached. Cross this and climb the steps up to the road. *Remember these steps.*

Here we make a short diversion to Lower Sapey. Turn left along the road to reach, at the top of the hill, the picturesque, medieval Sapey

Church of St Bartholomew, Lower Sapey

Court (at which you can only peer over the hedge) and the fascinating Lower Sapey Church of St Bartholomew which is usually open.

Through the Churches Conservation Trust much of the church has been restored with great skill and delicacy. There is an interesting pamphlet available in the church describing their on-going work. The floor is a new earth floor to match the original one. In order to help compact it we are encouraged 'please feel free to stamp your feet'!

Having done so let us return to the walk.

Now retrace your footsteps back down the hill to the steps where you turned off for Lower Sapey. Continue along the road past them, round the bend to cross Sapey Brook by a bridge. Here on your right by the house is a double sign on a single post. Ignore the more obvious bridle sign and follow the direction of the walking sign, going into the coppice and up very steeply to the left to a stile at the top.

The route now follows along the edge of the woods on your right, up the hill, swinging right over a stile and, still following the edge of the wood, to a gate in the far corner of the second field. Turn sharp right after the gate and down into the woods. Go sharp right again over a bridge and up to a field gate. Continuing up the hill leads to another gate and a further gate across a grassy track. Go straight on again, over the skyline, when Hill Farm (backed by a fine view of the Malverns) will suddenly appear in front. The gate to the left of the buildings will give access to the farm track.

Take a moment to admire both the aspect of the farm, the farm house itself, and the unusual long wooden barn near the stables.

To the very left of all the buildings a gate in the field fence gives access to the next field on the right.

Go diagonally right across this field to two gates in the far corner. Go through the right-hand metal gate, cross a short ridge between a dried up pond and a steep drop, to another gate. Beyond this go diagonally left up the hill to a gate between the woods and a hedge. Turn right beyond.

Keeping the hedge on your right continue to the top of the field, then left to skirt the house, coming to a road at a gate. Opposite there is a gate to the left and a stile to the right. Go over the stile and through a small coppice into a large field. Keep to the left side, down to the bottom of the field. A way through the hedge ahead leads across a footbridge into another large field.

The footpath is straight on, following a line parallel with telegraph poles on the right, to reach a gate in the left corner by Woodmanton Farm.

Many footpaths converge on Woodmanton Farm. Go straight through the farm, passing its main buildings on the right, to reach its metalled approach road and to experience the fine view to the east.

Turn right along this road and very soon turn left over a cattle grid and follow the track to Ayngstree along the top of the ridge with, in clear weather, more wonderful views of the Malverns ahead. At Ayngstree find a well-kept path to the left between the house and the field hedge. Ignoring a gate immediately on the left go down this path and through a small gate, then along the left side of the field. Keep on this line until, just after leaving the field, a well-defined sunken path to the left leads down through woods to a field gate and a sudden view southwards over Lower Tedney Farm

Keep to the left of the hillside (Tedney Bank) down to a gate which leads to a road. Turn right and walk along this for about half a mile. After passing Lower Tedney Farm and then two more left-side field boundaries a waymarked path, again on the left (and where the road swings right), crosses the middle of the next field to reach a line of woods.

The route goes steeply down into the woods to the River Teme. Follow to the right along the river, then out of the woods, across fields to a track which eventually passes a pumping station and becomes a concrete drive leading to Whitbourne.

Whitbourne is worth a few minutes pause with its church, Olde Rectory and the moated Whitbourne Court.

Swing right after the church, then almost immediately turn left through Whitbourne and Meadow Green to walk along the road three quarters of a mile back to the Wheatsheaf. The bus stop, if you want it, is beside the Whitbourne war memorial about a a quarter of a mile along the road. This road passes the delightfully named 'Live and Let Live' Inn at Meadow Green.

13
Kingsbury Waterways
by Horace Marsh

A circular walk featuring the numerous lakes comprising the renowned Kingsbury Water Park, the adjacent River Tame, and the Birmingham & Fazeley Canal. Take your binoculars!

Distance: 7 miles (11 km) or 5 miles (8 km).
Maps: Landranger 139; Pathfinder 913/914.
Car Parking: Visitor Centre (GR203960). Enter the Water Park by the main entrance in Bodymoor Heath Lane.
Public Transport: MRN Service 116 Birmingham/Tamworth.
To join the walk: *If arriving from Tamworth* cross the main A51 road at the pedestrian crossing and walk up the road on the left hand side of the White Swan car park to the bus stop where walkers *arriving from Birmingham* will alight. From this bus shelter turn left along the path which has the Heart of England Way waymark: this path runs along the right hand side of the recreational ground to the churchyard.
Walk to the right through a gap in the low rail and carry on along the road for about 25 metres, then bear left to walk down the path alongside and through the churchyard of Kingsbury Parish Church of St Peter and St Paul, keeping the church on the left. After passing Kingsbury Hall on the right descend a flight of steps to cross the footbridge over the River Tame. *Now start reading from* ✷ *on page 63.*
Start/Finish: Kingsbury Water Park Visitor Centre (GR203960).
Refreshments: Water Park Visitor Centre; Dog and Doublet pub, Curdworth; White Swan, Kingsbury.

WITH the Visitor Centre behind you walk forward, following a Centenary Way waymark and passing the car parking area on your right. Cross the road and follow a path under power lines with a grassy area on the right.

After about 100 metres the path divides: here take the left-hand fork signed Far Leys Car Park and continue over a footbridge. Almost immediately turn right and follow the path which runs between Bodymoor Heath Water on the right and Willows Pool on the left.

At the end of Willows Pool (marker post 34) turn left and walk diagonally across a meadow along a gravel path. Follow this path to its end to meet a crossing track. Turn right along the track and walk for about 50 metres to reach two marker posts (10 and 32). Turn right here and follow the path to reach a crossing path (post 15P). Turn left here and walk to the end where another path crosses.

For the shorter walk turn left over a footbridge and walk to another footbridge over the River Tame. Turn left here and now continue reading from ✴ on page 63.

Continuing with the longer walk go over the crossing path and walk

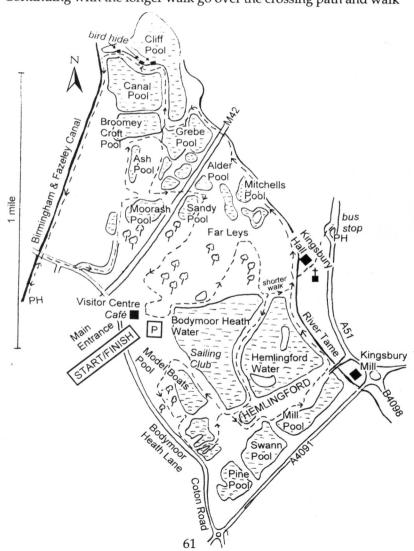

Kingsbury Water Park

The 600 acre Water Park is an attractive nature reservation with thirty lakes and pools, all interlinked by footpaths through woodlands, meadows, and along dams between the lakes, and bordered by the River Tame on one side, and the canal on the other side. The park caters for many types of leisure activities such as angling, canoeing, sailing, hydroplaning, model boating, cycling, birdwatching, orienteering, boardsailing, horse riding, cycling and walking.

The park which is owned and managed by Warwickshire County Council Countryside Service possesses a comprehensive Visitor Centre comprising a shop, audio visual exhibition, café and toilet facilities. Refreshments can be obtained between April and November. There is also a children's play area and several picnic sites throughout the park.

The Visitor Centre is well worth a call to view the various displays, and obtain relevant ·leaflets and booklets. It is also strongly recommended that you watch the free ten minute long film. This graphically publicises the history, natural features and activities of the park, and is normally continuous throughout the day, but if it is not running the staff will readily run it on request.

There are many paths through the park and these are liberally marked with colour coded and numbered posts and waymarks. You should not normally need to refer to these on this walk although in places they are mentioned where it has been thought that they would be helpful.

For more information about the Water Park telephone 01827 872660.

---

directly to a footbridge. Cross the footbridge and follow the path which runs along the long causeway between Hemlingford Water on the left and Bodymoor Heath Water on the right to the roadway at the end.

Turn right along the road and walk between Bodymoor Heath Water on the right and Causeway Pool on the left. Follow the road round to the right passing marker post 5 and continue walking along the road passing Bodymoor Heath Water, the Midlands Hydroplane Club and Tamworth Sailing Club on the right, and the Model Boating Pool on the left. Follow the road round to the left at the sailing club and walk for about 50 metres to a path on the left signposted 'Model Boat Club' and 'Nature Trail' and showing the Centenary Way waymark.

Turn left along this path, then immediately walk diagonally over to the entrance to the nature trail signed 'Nature Trail Start' and opened by Phil Drabble in 1990.

Join the nature trail and walk for about 100 metres to a kissing gate.

Ignoring the track to the right go through the gate and follow the trail until it reaches another kissing gate. Do not go through this but take the path to the right and follow this, passing between a pool and Bodymoor Heath Road, then between two pools to finally emerge in a grassy clearing at the rear of some farm buildings. Swing left across the grass, past a bench on the right, to a kissing gate at the end of the path. Go through the gate and turn right along the path ignoring the 'Nature Trail' sign.

Walk along the path to the road, cross over the road passing marker post 5 and a Centenary Way waymark, then walk diagonally across to rejoin the road. Walk ahead along the road for about 15 metres where a path on the right hand side will be seen. Still on the Centenary Way take this path, which skirts Causeway Pool on the left, then Swann Pool on the right, then carry on to the end of the path to emerge on to the road and a parking area at marker post 13.

Walk diagonally across the road and follow the path indicated by the Centenary Way waymark with Swann Pool on the right and Mill Pool on the left. Turn left at a small conifer plantation, then cross over a footbridge to follow the path along the dam on the left-hand side of Mill Pool. Continue to meet marker post 8. Turn left at the post to immediately reach a road where, just right of opposite, there is a hedge gap into a meadow. Go through the gap and walk straight ahead across the meadow parallel to the hedge on the right, with Hemlingford Water on the left: this lake is used for windsurfing.

Just before to reaching the river bridge a crossing bridleway will be met: turn left along this and walk with the River Tame on the right to reach the Kingsbury footbridge, identified by bridleway marker No 27.

You can now walk into Kingsbury, either to visit the White Swan for refreshment, or, if you have arrived by bus, to leave the walk. Turn right to cross the footbridge, then ascend the steps between Kingsbury Parish Church and Kingsbury Hall. Passing the churchyard on your right reach a road. Turn right along this for about 50 metres, then walk through a gap in the low railing and go down the left-hand side of the recreational ground to the road where the White Swan can be seen to the right. The return bus stop for Tamworth is immediately on the right. For Birmingham cross the road and walk right, around the White Swan, cross the road by the pedestrian crossing and go forward to the bus stop.

To continue with the walk after refreshment return through the churchyard and down the steps to cross the footbridge and turn right.

✱ Now follow the river bank downstream, passing Kingsbury Hall to the right.

Kingsbury Hall was originally a hunting lodge for the Mercian Kings ruling from Tamworth in the eighth century. The name Kingsbury is derived from this, since Bury is the Saxon name for a fortified manor house, thus this lodge became the King's fortified manor house. The house was later rebuilt in the twelfth century as a hall for the Bracebridge family and was modified to its present form in the fifteenth century, it is now a farmhouse.

You soon pass on the right hand side of Mitchell Pool which is used by canoes, inflatable dinghies and rafts. Continue walking along the river-bank and, ignoring a turn left direction post (marker 29), walk to a footbridge. Cross this and immediately turn sharp right to follow the course of the river to the three span M42 motorway bridge.

Walk under the centre span of the bridge, still following the river-bank and passing Grebe Pool on the left. At the end of this pool, and just before the river bends sharply to the right, turn sharp left and continue walking along the side of the pool to reach a T-junction of paths. Grebe Pool is a natural pool, not used by fishermen, and supports a wide variety of fish, water fowl and plant life.

At the T-junction take the right hand path, now walking along the dam with Cliff Pool on the right, to another T-junction of paths. Turn right at this point with a post stating 'Walkers Only' and walk beside the dam between Broomey Croft Pool on the left and Cliff Pool on the right (ignoring a fisherman's path on the left) and continuing past the end of the dam until the path swings left, passing a bird hide on the right.

Cliff Pool is part of a Nature Reservation and an embankment was specially constructed to screen the wild fowl from human disturbance. Since it is inaccessible to visitors the only way the wild fowl and wading birds can be observed is from three hide shelters sited along the pool bank These are very popular with birdwatchers and are well worth visiting especially with binoculars. Typical of the wild fowl are mallard, heron, wigeon, great crested grebe, and tufted duck: the wading birds include green, wood and common sandpipers, dunlin, ruff, woodcock, curlew, spotted redshank, lapwing, golden plover and oystercatcher. Broomey Croft and Canal Pools are mainly used by anglers, with pike and carp being the two largest species.

Continue along the path, passing more bird hides on the right, and on reaching the Birmingham & Fazeley Canal turn left and and walk along the causeway between the canal and Canal Pool as far as a low log barrier. Pass the barrier onto the canal towpath and continue in a southerly direction past Curdworth Bottom Lock No 11, with its integral swing bridge, and Curdworth Common Lock No 10 until Bodymoor Heath Bridge is reached.

At this point if either food or liquid refreshment is required continue along the canal for about 400 metres to a delightful canalside pub, the Dog and Doublet, where hot meals, sandwiches, hot and cold drinks can be obtained. After this welcome break return along the canal to the far side of Bodymoor Heath Bridge to rejoin the walk.

The Birmingham & Fazeley Canal, authorised in 1874, was originally built as a junction canal to link Birmingham with the south-east. Its main purpose was to carry coal from the Midland pits to the industrial Midlands, and gravel for the construction industry.

Leave the towpath by walking up the exit path on to Bodymoor Heath Lane. Continue walking for about 200 metres along the road, passing Bodymoor Heath Methodist Church on the left, until the Broomey Croft entrance to the Kingsbury Water Park is reached on the left hand side of the road.

Turn left into this entrance and walk straight down the lane, ignoring the left hand minor road junction marked 'Welcome to Kingsbury Water Park' encountered after about 100 metres. Continue down the lane and follow it through a left bend for about 500 metres until further progress is prevented by the Park administration and maintenance complex. At this dead end turn right and walk down a track alongside the cottage named Moorash Farm for about 50 metres to reach a gap in the hedge on the left where a fenced path will be found. Follow this short path to emerge on to a lane.

Turn right along the lane, passing the camping ground on the left and the small Ash Pool on the right. Continue walking down the road as far as Broomey Croft Pool and car-park, then turn right, past the toilets, along the Heart of England Way path for about 100 metres to a junction of paths. Turn right and walk for another 100 metres, then turn right again, still on the Heart of England Way, passing Gibsons Pool on the left and the Rare Breeds Farm on the right. Follow the path to Moorash Pool (marker post 8).

Turn left along the crossing path and walk to the M42 bridge, passing Gibsons Pool and Burdetts Pool on the left and Moorash Pool and Sandy Pool on the right. Carry on under the motorway until the first path on the right is reached, then turn right to follow this path alongside Sandy Pool on the right. Continue walking to a fork in the path, then, taking the right fork, pass marker post 4 on the left and follow the path around, going through a 'Watch Group Conservation' area.

When the path reaches the road, turn right to cross a bridge, then follow the road to the Visitor Centre.

If you arrived by bus now continue reading from the start on page 60.

14
Around Draycote Water

by Roger Gibbs

This walk circumnavigates Draycote Water which lies between Coventry, Rugby and Southam. It features a number of small, delightful Warwickshire villages, conservation areas and waymarked fieldpaths. The Ramblers' Association campaign for greater public access deserves all the support it can get, and during this walk some of the issues will be evident.

Distance: 9-10 miles (14.5-16 km)
Maps: Landranger 140/151; Pathfinder 977/956
Car Parking: 1) Draycote Water Country Park (GR465692). Open 8.00 a.m. to sunset (pay and display); 2) Lay-by on A426 (GR468684)
Public Transport: Stagecoach service 63, Leamington Spa/Rugby, passes Draycote Water
Start/Finish: Draycote Water Country Park (GR466692)
Refreshments: Leam Valley Country Café on A426
Useful telephone numbers:
   Severn Trent Water Authority, Warden' Office (for permission to walk the reservoir's perimeter road): Rugby 811107.
   Draycote Water. Fishing Lodge 01788-812018; Warden's office 01788-811107.

O UR WALK starts from the entrance to Draycote Water Country Park. If you are planning to complete the walk be sure to take some refreshments as opportunities to purchase any are rare until the end of the day.

Any children with you should be deterred from running over to the nearby play area, attractive as it may appear. There will be an opportunity to take full advantage of the facilities at the end of the walk if time and energy permit.

Make your way along the access road, generally due west, and look ahead for a kissing gate as the road turns left. Go through the gate and climb the hill to the trig point at the top.

Notice the windsock on the right, and then the first sighting of the reservoir. This was constructed for the storage of water pumped from the River Leam for flood control, for water level control and for supply to Rugby and Leamington. It was completed in 1970 and covers 600 acres to a depth of up to 65 feet.

Unless you have dogs with you it is well worth making a short diversion to the waterside picnic areas. From the trig point cross the hilltop car park and follow the path down to the right as indicated by the notice 'No dogs at water's edge'. The path goes left to a kissing gate and out onto the shoreline. Proceed along the shore (no swimming!) until you reach the gate and fence.

What a pity! No public access beyond this point! So, make your way back along the road, through the gate, and back up to the car park at the top of the hill. Dogs can now continue!

This is Hensborough Hill, an excellent viewpoint at 370 feet above sea level, 65 feet above reservoir level.

Now return to the Country Park entrance by following the access road from the hilltop. As you cross the main field observe the ridges and furrows that were formed by strip farming some centuries ago, and which indicate that the field has not been ploughed in more recent times, being used, probably, for grazing. During the walk watch out for several other excellent examples of such ridge and furrow evidence. As you can read at the information board, the normal length of each strip is one furlong, and the width one perch (5½ yards), giving an area of one rood (¼ acre).

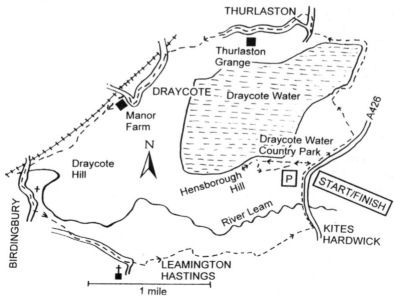

Because there is no public access to the boundary road around Draycote Water we now have to walk along the main A426 for half a mile. Leave the Country Park and walk to the main road in an easterly direction. Bear left at the main road and use the verge if possible to avoid the traffic.

After a quarter of a mile we reach a streamside footpath that crosses the road. A signpost and stiles clearly mark access to the path.

Use the stile in the hedge on the left, taking care to notice that we are crossing a ditch by way of a plank bridge. Don't step off the side! – this is easy to do if overgrown. Follow the stream, heading north-west with the stream on the right, along two fields, over a waymarked stile in the hedge that crosses the path, to arrive at a double stile and bridge across the stream in the corner of the second field.

Turn right across this bridge and over the stiles to join a clear path ahead with a hedge on the left and woodland to the right. At the end of this short straight, follow the waymarks and hedge to the right, and then to the left, passing the Severn Trent workings – not exactly the sort of 'waterside' we had in mind but, nevertheless, an essential part of modern living!

To the south you should be able to see some high ground. This is Beacon Hill and Napton on the Hill, some six or seven miles distant.

The way is clear, a double hedged green track on the left. Two horse

Thurlaston village

jumps up this path we arrive at a field gate with a clearly waymarked stile on the left. Take this path down, with lovely views of the water, and of the windmill at Thurlaston. Follow the path to the right and over another stile out onto the open field. Follow the line of the hedge on your left, over a couple of stiles, and into some trees, passing a reedy willowed pool on the right.

A fingerpost now points the way to the left, over a stile, a footbridge, and out onto the boundary road. 'No public access'. 'Contractors only'!

The public right of way is indicated ahead, keeping the hedge on the left. We are now heading west towards the village of Thurlaston. Notice the ridge and furrow as the path curves gently to find a stile in the corner of the field, footpath straight on, over a stream, through a kissing gate, and straight ahead up the concrete road to come out by the church.

Maintain the same direction past the thatched 'Rose Cottage' to the T-junction where we go right. Thurlaston was the 'Best Kept Small Village' for 1985-86 and must be a contender for more up-to-date awards.

Take the second left at the stocks down the appropriately named Stocks Lane, to a small conservation area. Notice, to the right, the encased water pump marked WK 1850.

Two footpaths leave the conservation area. Ours is to the left over a wooden stile. The path is clear on the ground as we follow it to emerge onto the metalled road. Keep in the same direction and follow the road.

Old water pump in Thurlaston

After about half a mile (past Thurlaston Grange) the road becomes a track, but the way is clear, prompted by blue waymarks, the colour indicating bridleway status (as opposed to yellow for footpaths). After passing through the golf course the bridle-way progresses through a series of gates until emerging into a meadow that has been classified as a nature reserve. Look out for cowslips, orchids, yellow-rattle, and other floral delights depending on the time of year.

The way is evident as it leaves the hedge-line, as is the ridge and furrow effect, emphasised by the patterns of buttercups and daisies (when in flower!).

And so out onto the lane, bearing left to Draycote village. Follow the lane into the village and round the sharp bend to the right. The lane then bends left and right again towards the railway arch over the road. Some yards before this arch a footpath marker indicates our way to the left.

The path now follows the general direction of the railway line which is indicated by the clear tree line over to the right.

Look out for a wicket gate in the hedge straight ahead across the field (south-west), and aim for it across the middle of the field. Go through the waymarked gate into a field and follow the field edge on the left. When the field edge veers off to the left, and as we are now no longer alongside a hedge, the exact line of the path is not now obvious in this large field. However, there is no difficulty as it generally follows the line of the stream in a south-westerly direction, maintaining a distance of 50 yards or so from it.

Ahead we can see the end of the field, a fence with trees each side of a central clear area. The stile lies about halfway between the stream and the clear area, and is indicated by two or three isolated trees close to the corner of the field, but within the field.

The stile to be climbed lies over a wet area – which should be negotiated with care if you want to avoid soggy socks – as you enter the meadow ahead through which a farm drive curves.

A waymark post ahead shows the route, straight across the drive and around a pool in the centre of the field. Bear right to the metal gates which indicate the exit from the field to the lane. Turn left along the lane, over the River Leam, and head up to Birdingbury. Passing the church on the left we very soon observe the open countryside and the inevitable 'Legal proceedings will be taken against trespassers'. Take the next left (at the bus shelter) down a short lane. Where the lane turns right look for the footpath straight on between two houses. The footpath runs parallel to the drive of the newer house, and left of it, indicated by slabs on the ground fenced on both sides.

The path goes over a stile into a field, maintaining a south-easterly direction, and crossing more ridges and furrows, through two field gates (the second being the right-most of two), and ends in the far right corner of the field, at the point where the lane crosses the stream.

Back out in the lane we go left to Leamington Hastings. As we enter the village there is a sharp right turn in the lane. We, however, go straight on down the lane marked 'No through road' which bears left after about 100 yards. Look out for the footpath sign taking us down a narrow track between houses to arrive at a stile and out into an open field. Following the waymark we turn right onto a clear track along the edge of the field with the hedge on our right.

Now going due east we go straight on to the corner of the field where another hedge joins us from the left. Hedges on both sides now guide us to a stile and waymark directly ahead. The hedge is now on the left and remains so as we follow it to the right and then left to cross a stream. A series of stiles and waymarks now is encountered that take us across a number of fields.

Keep the hedge on the left until you emerge into an open field. The path lies straight ahead and is indicated by a lone marker post up ahead. Turn right at this post and then left to cross a stile and then another stream where we turn right and then left. We now have a hedge on our right after which we come into a long paddock, at the end of which can be seen some houses. Walk the length of the paddock to a gate which leads to a lane and onto the main road, the A426. *If you are using public transport you can catch the Stagecoach 63 bus here.*

Otherwise turn left and walk along the main road until you reach the clearly signposted road back to Draycote Water on the left, in just over half a mile, passing the Cherry Tree Chinese Restaurant on the left and the Leam Valley Golf Centre and Country Café on the right.

You will recognise the Country Park and can now allow the use of the playground, time and energy permitting.

If possible, pay a visit to Dunchurch, a couple of miles up the A426. The Green Man serves an excellent range of beers, and has a table skittle alley. The Dun Cow Hotel was being re-developed at the time of writing, but on 23 December 1837, George Stephenson and his son Robert dined there to celebrate the completion of the Kilsby tunnel on the Birmingham to London Railway, for which Robert was the engineer. George and Robert were the first two presidents of the Institution of Mechanical Engineers.

15
Henley

by Bob Knowles

Starting and finishing at Henley-in-Arden these two walks follow the River Alne and the Stratford-upon-Avon Canal for part of their route. Both walks visit Preston Bagot church and pass the site of a Norman castle at Beaudesert. Henley itself has a High Street almost a mile long and is a living museum of English domestic architecture. The longer walk also passes through part of the village of Langley with some picturesque cottages, and a lovely pool at Yarningale Common.

Distance: 8¾ miles (14 km) or 5¼ miles (8.5 km).
Maps: Landranger 151; Pathfinder 975.
Car Parking: At Henley, off Warwick Road (GR152662).
Public Transport: Stagecoach service X20 (Birmingham/Stratford), or British Rail, to Henley.
Start/Finish: High Street, Henley (GR151660).
Refreshments: Pubs and cafés at Henley.

L EAVE Henley-in-Arden by walking south along the High Street towards Stratford. Cross Warwick Road at the traffic lights, near the Golden Cross pub, and then cross a bridge over a small brook – a tributary of the River Alne that we shall shortly be following during the first section of our walk. After a further 250 metres turn left over a stile and walk across a school playing field to a stile in the opposite fence. Having climbed the stile follow the footpath over two footbridges to Blackford Mill. As you emerge from the path turn left and pass in front of the old mill, now converted into a house. Pass through a gate and turn right through a second gate into a field. Walk with the hedge on your right until you reach the River Alne.

Follow the river through three fields until having just passed under an electricity line you reach a stile, a wicket gate and a footbridge. From here turn half left and walk diagonally across the field towards a stile at the left of a line of trees, keeping the cottage over to your left. If you look to your right from this path you may catch a glimpse of Wootton Pool which is the immediate destination of the river we have been following.

The stile will take you into a lane where you should turn right and cross a stream, also on its way to the grounds of Wootton Hall. Turn left onto a drive and follow the line of the stream until the drive turns right.

72

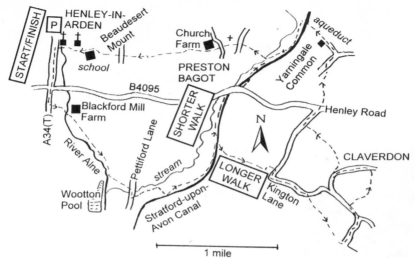

In front is the site of a moated house, the outline of which can be clearly seen. Turn right with the drive and follow it past Canal Cottage to the bridge over the Stratford-upon-Avon Canal.

Turn left onto the towpath and follow it until you reach a split cast iron bridge, number 49. These bridges were erected in 1815 when this section of the Stratford Canal was constructed. Unlike the more costly type of bridge, under which the towpath passes, the horse would make his way around these, so requiring a slot for the towrope to pass through.

For the longer walk now continue reading from ✱ below.

For the shorter walk follow the towpath for a further 1¼ kilometres, passing under two road bridges and crossing with the towpath to the other side of the canal. When the path returns to the left bank you have reached the point at which you rejoin the longer walk. Cross the bridge and continue straight on to a public footpath which turns right to a footbridge. Now continue reading from ❸ on page 76.

✱ Taking the longer walk now cross bridge 49 and turn right down a few steps to the public footpath. You will find yourself in the corner of a field and you should walk diagonally across (SSE) to the gate in the opposite corner. Pass through the gate onto what used to be a track, with hedges on both sides, to the farm that you see ahead. Sadly the hedges are now gone and you must walk in as straight a line as possible toward the farm buildings, keeping to the right of the electricity line pole. From the top of the slight rise you will see a gate that gives access to what is

Split bridge on the Stratford Canal

left of the track between a hedge and a fence. Follow the track through another gate and turn through a gate on the left. Then climb a stile and walk forward 50 metres, following the fence on your right, and at the end of the fence turn right and walk to a stile that can be seen in the hedge opposite. This will take you into Kington Lane.

Turn right and follow the lane past Kington Grange with its ancient barn, several cottages and the new development of Kington Rise. After about a kilometre on the lane you will pass Kington Cottage Farm on your right. Following this, the lane starts to bend to the left, and a stile onto a public footpath will be seen on the right.

Cross the stile and follow the path over a drive and straight on with a garden fence on your right, through a small wooded area, and out into meadows, which in spring and early summer are full of wild flowers. Walk with the hedge on your left through the meadows until you reach a stile. Climb this onto a track that will lead you via another stile out into a lane at Langley.

Turn left and walk up the lane past some very picturesque cottages. When you reach a junction signed left to Claverdon take this road almost to the top of the hill.

Just past a drive to a house (The White House) on the right is a footpath over a stile beside a gate. This path will take you down to a further gate and stile that leads to a field. Opposite is yet another gate and stile, following which the path runs downhill to the right of the hedge, through a gate and down to a footbridge over a stream.

Continue on over the bridge and out into a field, over a stile and, keeping to the left of the hedge, up a steep hill. At the top it is worth stopping, not only to catch your breath, but to turn round for a splendid view over the Warwickshire countryside. Continue to follow the fence until you reach a stile to a lane.

Turn left along the lane and walk about half a kilometre until just before the drive on the right to Woodside B&B you will see a stile with a notice informing you that there may be race horses in the field.

Climb the stile and turn right across open ground, making for the rounded corner of the fence to the left of a gate. Walk with the fence on your right and climb the stile in the corner of the field. The stile will take you onto a short path through some trees to a further stile that leads out into a field.

Ignore the waymarked path that leads straight on, turn half left and walk to the brow of the hill from where you will see a stile to the right of a tree in the hedge at the bottom of the hill. Over the stile turn right and go over another stile beside a gate, then turn half left and cross the field diagonally to the opposite corner.

Pass through a gate and turn left, go over a stile and continue straight on until you reach a farm drive. Turn right and walk towards the gate. Just before reaching it go left as indicated out onto a drive that runs to a nursery.

Turn left and follow the drive to its junction with a lane where you should turn right and walk to the T-junction with the main Henley Road.

On the other side of the main road you will see a small square building: take the path over a stile to the right of this. Walk with the hedge on your left through a further gate and on until the hedge turns sharp left away from you. Continue on, bearing to the right towards a building, the roof of which you can see through the hedge in front. Look for a waymarker arrow fixed to a tree pointing down a bank to a footbridge.

Cross the stream and follow the path straight ahead over a stile and out onto a lane. Turn right along the lane, pausing long enough to admire the delightful pool on the left, just before reaching Yarningale Common.

Turn left onto the common and cut across to the lane (Yarningale Lane), turn left again and follow the lane until you reach its end and are confronted by a house. Pass to the right of this and follow the path up some steps which return us to the Stratford Canal beside an aqueduct over a stream. Go left along the canal and cross the bridge to Bucket Lock Cottage.

Like many cottages along this canal it has a semi-circular roof, suggesting that the materials used in its construction were formerly employed to support the arch of a nearby bridge until it was completed.

Follow the towpath south past two locks to the point at which it crosses to the other side of the canal, but do not cross the bridge.

Turn right onto a public footpath which bends to the right through woods to a footbridge.

○ *Here the shorter walk rejoins the longer one.*

Cross the stream and continue on to a stile. Having climbed this go forward to the hedge on the far side of the field. Go along on the right of the hedge until you reach a gate in the corner. Cross the next field to a stile which you will see about 50 metres to the left of a gate in the opposite hedge. This leads to a lane and on the other side you will see a path that leads to a church.

This is All Saints, the parish church of Preston Bagot. It's a charming old church with a shingled bell tower and well worth a look round if it is open (which, sadly, is not very often). Outside, to the left of the door,

is the tomb of one John Shakespeare (d. 1840). Who knows? Perhaps a descendant of the Bard himself. After all, we are only a bike ride away from Stratford!

Leave the churchyard by a kissing gate and turn right. Go through another kissing gate under an oak tree: on the right is an old bench with a now indecipherable inscription which I believe used to read 'Rest and be Thankful'.

Follow the path downhill, cross the lane and go through a gate. Walk with the hedge on your right to a stile, climb this, go straight across a narrow field and over a stile. Again with a

Church of All Saints, Preston Bagot

hedge on your right walk to another stile. Cross this and go straight forward across the next field to a stile at the right of a tree. Ignore the stile on your right and continue with the hedge on your right through three more fields, then straight across a field to a stile and onto a path. Turn right and after 20 metres turn left over a stile. Keeping to the left of the hedge continue on until you reach Edge Lane and turn right.

Take the footpath immediately on your left and follow it forward to the end of the field, turn right over a wide stile and left over a second into woods. Walk down the steps and a slope into a recreation ground, cross to the gate opposite and follow the path between the houses. Continue on this public footpath across a road, turn right and follow the path round a school.

Once the path has turned left Beaudesert Mount, the site of a Norman castle, is on your right and may be visited. It was once owned by the powerful de Montford family until Simon de Montford was killed at the Battle of Evesham, when it was burnt to the ground.

Reaching the end of a cul-de-sac continue forward along the path and you will emerge onto a lane with the Church of St Nicholas on your right, which has a Norman door and chancel. After a visit to this ancient place of worship continue along the lane, passing over the same stream along which our walk started, to the High Street.

Before you leave Henley, try a well-earned Henley ice cream and take some time to look at the High Street, which is almost a mile long and has an example of nearly every type of English domestic architecture.

Henley. The Manor House

16
The Alne Valley
by Elizabeth Claydon

This twelve mile walk (which can be reduced to six miles) passes through some of Warwickshire's loveliest countryside. The starting point is the beautiful Saxon church at Wootton Wawen, on the A34 Birmingham-Stratford Road, once an old turnpike coaching route. Walking southward from here, through water meadows beside the Alne, brings us to Aston Cantlow, with its fifteenth century Guildhall and its church where Shakespeare's parents were married. From here, the routes divide, and follow undulating paths over the Rough Hills, to join the Stratford-upon-Avon Canal at Newnham, which will take us back over the longest cast-iron canal aqueduct in England.

Distance: 12 miles (19 km)or 6 miles (9.5 km).
Maps: Landranger 150 and 151; Pathfinder 975 and 997
Car Parking: Beside the village hall, at the start of the B4089, GR151632.
Public Transport: Bus: Stagecoach X20, Birmingham/Stratford. Alight at Wootton Wawen.
Train: Birmingham/Stratford. Alight at Wootton Wawen (request stop). From the station walk east to reach the Bulls Head, then turn right on the A3400 to reach the starting point.
Start/Finish: St. Peter's Church, Wootton Wawen. GR153633.
Refreshments: Pubs at Wootton Wawen, Aston Cantlow and Great Alne; Grocer, Post Office at Wootton Wawen.

OUR WAY lies down the narrow lane beside the pillar box, marked as a public footpath, opposite the driveway to St. Peter's Church. It is worth visiting the church here, which dates back to Anglo-Saxon times and is considered to be one of the finest in the county. There is much of interest, including brasses, a chained library, and an eighteenth century clock mechanism.

Follow this quiet lane down to the kissing-gate at the end, and pass through into the field, keeping straight ahead on the clearly defined raised path until it meets the River Alne.

Continue along the river bank, with the Alne on your left, until a stile is reached. This waterside is lined with a mass of blackthorn during April and May. Go over the stile, and turn back momentarily to look at St. Peter's Church tower.

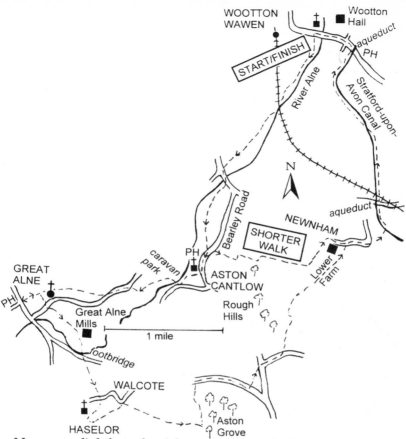

Now veer slightly to the right, and over another stile at the start of a row of conifers. Continue as before, keeping the river on your left and a wire fence on your right. Go through a kissing gate on the right of a large oak, and then go directly ahead across a large field, making for the railway bridge on the far right-hand side. Pass through the metal gate, and out onto the lane.

Turn sharp right, under the railway bridge, to meet the Alne again as it re-appears on your left-hand side. Continue for about 75 yards until the river swings away from the lane, and at about 20 yards from this point reach a stile on the left. Cross this into the field, and set off to the stile immediately ahead; over again – and across to another stile in the opposite corner, sited between a farm on the left, and a picturesque thatched cottage on the right. Once out onto the lane turn left.

On the left is Grey Mill Farm, the first of the three mills that we shall see, following the longer walk, along the Alne Valley. At one time a ford existed here.

Walk just a few yards to cross a waymarked footbridge on the right, into a field again. The way is easy to follow. Aim for the top of the hill, at an angle of about 45 degrees, to cross the stile about half-way along the hedge, with a vista of Arden opening up before us, and the first sighting of Aston Cantlow, our immediate destination. Descend towards the left of the buildings in the valley ahead of you, over a stile, and across another field, to emerge on the B4089 by a stile, close to a 'dangerous bend' road sign, displaying four chevrons.

Turn left along the road, following the sign for Aston Cantlow. Cross the River Alne, and just over the bridge, on the right-hand side, go through a gate and along a public footpath through low-lying meadows, edged with willows, to Aston Cantlow. During the spring and summer, look out for butterflies, swallows, swifts and dragonflies along here.

Keep the hedge on the left, pass through a gate, and then, when the end of the hedge is reached, veer left to a clearly waymarked stile, enabling you to cross the dismantled railway line from Alcester to Bearley Halt. In days gone by this linked the Evesham line with the Stratford line. Bearing right, alongside a fence, make your way out onto the lane, known as Chapel Lane, through the houses, and turn right into Aston Cantlow's main street, where a neat row of nineteenth century cottages will greet you.

Between Cantella Farm and The Old Forge a glimpse of uneven ground marks what was once the site of a medieval castle, built near the river by St Thomas Cantelupe (the only villager in Warwickshire to become a saint and from whose name Cantlow is derived). Continuing along the street two half-timbered buildings come into view. On the left is the fifteenth century Guildhall, and on the right is the fourteenth century Kings Head Inn, where the wedding breakfast of Shakespeare's parents took place.

Just past the King's Head turn into Church Lane on the right and take the footpath through the lych-gate to see the thirteenth century church of St. John the Baptist, with Perpendicular tower, where it is believed John Shakespeare married Mary Arden in 1557. The church has a late fourteenth century clock made by a blacksmith from the village, and also a fifteenth century font.

It is at this point that the long walk and the short walk separate. If you are doing the longer walk now continue reading from ✱ *on page 81*

Shorter walk: To reach Newnham and the return along the Stratford-upon-Avon Canal retrace your steps through the village, passing the end of Chapel Lane, and follow the Bearley Road until a 30 m.p.h. speed limit sign appears, alongside the last bungalow on the right-hand side, called 'Pear Tree Gardens'.

Here turn into the waymarked track and walk with the fence on the left. Go through a wide, open gateway, to follow the track as it turns left, then right. Pass between two gateposts and begin a steady climb, through an archway of ash and hawthorn, to a viewpoint at the top showing Aston Cantlow down below in the Alne Valley, with Lodge Hill, Round Hill and Badbury Hill beyond.

The Kings Head, Aston Cantlow

An extremely tall hedge on the left now shelters the track, as it continues across an open field, laced with buttercups in summer. Leave the protection of the hedge, crossing the next large field, aiming for the hedge opposite. Lower Farm, at Newnham, comes into view on the left. On reaching the hedge turn left along the near side of the hedge into Newnham, where a tarmac road begins, level with the first house in the village, 'Fairfield'. Follow this road past houses to rejoin the longer walk as, just past Tufnells Hill Farm, it comes in along a track from the right.

Now continue the shorter walk by reading from ✪ on page 85

✱ The longer walk continues straight ahead from the church porch, down the path beside the old school, built in 1848 by William Butterfield, now, sadly, like so many village schools, no more, to follow an easy fenced pathway which eventually reaches a lane. Turn right through a wooden gate where the sound of rushing water will guide you over a footbridge beside a sluice, a few yards to the left of the vehicle entrance to a caravan park. Here you will be reunited with the Alne.

Keep straight ahead, past the toilets on your left and a telephone kiosk on your right, to cross another branch of the Alne. A choice of two footpaths appears, but the one to the left is our course, and is followed easily, past a stile and over a footbridge into a large field. At this point, aim for the right of the pair of power poles. By now our stile will be coming into view, set in the right-hand corner. Follow yellow arrows along the old Alcester to Bearley line, here passing through a cutting, emerging on an old by-road, with splendid views of Oversley Wood ahead, truly magnificent in bluebell time.

Turn right now, to touch briefly on the busier B4089 and, turning left, walk facing the traffic for a distance of approximately 250 yards. Look out on your right-hand side for the private road to Maudsley and turn into it. A few steps along, diagonally cross a field on your left, passing beside a cricket field, to reach a woodland path. From the peace and tranquillity of this pathway it comes as quite a surprise to look out on the right at a factory building used in the manufacture of transmissions for the heavy vehicle industry. It was the target for several unsuccessful bomb attacks during the last war; now only the bomb craters remain in the Alne Hills nearby, as a last vestige of those troubled times.

After about a quarter of a mile a quiet residential roadway is reached. Cross over, and go a little to the right, and then down a wide footpath in the same direction, alongside gardens, until the open fields are reached again. Go through two kissing gates in succession, and into the churchyard of St. Mary Magdalene at Great Alne. (*Although visitors to the churchyard are welcome, a notice here points out that the path through the churchyard is not a right of way. The actual right of way passes to the right of the churchyard and leads to the B4089 near the Mother Huff Cap pub.*)

At this point, a choice is possible; the walk continues from the church porch. However, the Mother Huff Cap pub, named after the head on the beer, is the only place where food and drinks are obtainable in the village, so if these are required follow the sloping path to the right of the church porch to pass through a kissing gate onto a field path. Turn left, to follow this out onto the road, once the ancient Salt Way, and to your left again is the front entrance of the old seventeenth century coaching inn.

Twix Michaelmas and Martinmas
Old dame began to brew
First she brewed some old beer,

Then she brewed some new.
The first to pour was cloudy beer
But next there came the crystal clear
Then she brewed some more like that,
And on the top was Huff the Cap.
(Anon)

Retrace your steps back along the same route to our point of reference, the church porch. Follow the path down to the left from here, to come out on the B4089 again, beside an enormous horse chestnut tree which provides welcome shade on a hot day. Cross over the road, and turn right for a few paces, to join a field path on the left, through a kissing gate; walk straight across and over a stile bearing a green marker.

Proceed to the right-hand corner to find a gate to take you into the next field. Veer slightly left towards a kissing gate, about 20 yards to the right of a large oak, then continue forward to a stile beside another oak tree, 20 yards to the left of buildings. This brings you out onto the approach road to Great Alne Mills, which were working until 1963. This is the second mill that we pass by on our journey. The area also made a contribution to the flax industry, based at Alcester.

Turn right along this road, and right again across the front of the building. At the end of the building, turn immediately left towards some tennis courts. Follow the path, now waymarked, round the corner behind the trees to the footbridge near a weir on the River Alne again. Cross over the lane, turn left for a few paces, then turn right up some steps and through a gate into a field where, opposite, Haselor Church at the top of the hill comes into view. Carry straight on with a fence on the left, over a footbridge and two stiles.

Ignoring a path waymarked to the right, continue forward with the fence on your left to another stile. As early in the year as January, snowdrops grow beside the path here. Keeping by the hedge, cross over the next stile and out onto the lane. Cross the lane to veer right for the climb up the tarmac path to the church of St Mary and All Saints, Haselor, which stands at approximately 220 feet in an isolated situation, only approachable on foot, mid-way between the villages of Upton and Walcote. The tower is thirteenth century.

Nearing the top, on the right of the footpath, you will see the base of the original village cross, destroyed during the Reformation. The uneven ground nearby suggests that a small village existed here and was presumably abandoned after the Black Death.

Just beyond the sundial, near the church porch, a kissing-gate leads out of the churchyard into the field. Follow the yellow arrow to the left, staying close to the hedge, and cross the stile ahead. Still keep left, close to a fence on the left. Go through a gate and swing left, aiming to the right of barns ahead.

Go through two gates with a footbridge between them and, keeping a fence on the left, make for a stile at the top of the field. Cross this, go through a gate on the left and onto tarmac. Stay with this for about 15 yards before turning right, to meet a waymarked stile that will take you over into another field. During April cowslips flourish on this corner. Cross this field, keeping the hedge on the right, to the stile opposite.

Possibly your walk across here will coincide with the launching of a hot-air balloon from the nearby ballooning centre. Keeping in the same direction, cross two more stiles. The path begins to curve to the right, and on going through a gateway beside the remains of a third stile the waymarked ascent to Withycombe Wood begins. Follow the hedge on your left up to the stile in the fence, and once over, continue forward a few paces, to turn left on a woodland path. Spring opens a treasure chest of bluebells, primroses and orchids here, and buzzards can be seen circling overhead. (On one of my walks through here, a buzzard dropped its prey on the path in front of me.)

After a short distance, of approximately 200 yards, the path leaves Withycombe Wood and turns sharply to the left, following along the edge of a field, with the hedge on the right. Continue left from the corner, along the next side of the field, and through a gap in the hedge on the right in the next corner, and out onto the road.

Turn right, and walk along the road for about half a mile until, near power lines and just before the house 'Woodside' on the right, a waymarked stile appears in the hedge on the left-hand side. This path will take you straight on through the field, and out onto a road on the other side. Cross over, and follow the Wilmcote road ahead for a short distance, past Aston Holdings Farm, to reach a small white bridge over a stream.

About 50 yards further on leave the road, by a new waymarked gate on the left (ignoring the adjacent stile), beginning a well maintained footpath, climbing up hill, between two fields separated from each other by a ditch. A stile at the top brings you out onto some high ground known as the Rough Hills. This is a good vantage point for watching the sun go down, whatever the time of year. Looking in a westerly direction, the Alne Hills come into view.

The path, now a track, becomes fenced off and eventually weaves a zigzag route around a site of special scientific interest on the right, managed by the Nature Conservancy Council. This area was once the site of the old Newnham quarries, which produced lias stone used in the building of Alcester Town Hall, and also in 1546 for the repair of Clopton Bridge at Stratford-upon-Avon, and in 1694 for the rebuilding of St. Mary's Church, Warwick.

Continue through the gate ahead, and around the field edge, following waymark signs, and keeping the hedge on the right. Aim down towards the green barn ahead of you, through a metal gate just beyond this, and onto a wide, unsurfaced by-road, leading into the hamlet of Newnham.

Newnham consists of three farms, and several cottages with interesting gardens. When the quarry was working there was a population of about 300 here. Turn right into a road at the end of the track.

❍ *The shorter route and the long route now merge for the final waterside walk along the canal.*

Carry on forward until the road swings sharply to the left. Ignore this, and take the footpath ahead over a stile, bearing diagonally left across two fields, crossing a stile and then another in the corner of the field. Turn right, through bushes, into a field and then walk with a hedge on the left until the bottom of the field is reached. Continue round the corner for a few yards and pass through an opening in the hedge to find Draper Bridge, and the Stratford-upon-Avon Canal.

Cross the bridge, numbered 57, and turn left along the towpath. Built in 1816, the Stratford Canal cost £400,000, and is 26 miles long. By 1937 it had fallen into decline and it was not until restoration work was carried out by the National Trust, from 1960 to 1964, that it became a navigable waterway again. The original canal, known for its barrel-roofed cottages, had 46 locks, one tunnel, and three aqueducts. We shall see two of the aqueducts and a pair of locks on our return to Wootton Wawen.

Soon a converted canalside cottage is passed on the opposite bank, and just beyond the longest cast-iron canal aqueduct in England is reached, designed by William Whitmore in 1813, and extending 479 feet. At a maximum height of 33 feet, the towpath continues beside it, the full 14-span structure supported by thirteen brick piers, whilst below can be seen a section of the North Warwickshire Railway near Bearley.

Past Bearley Lock, No. 39 and approaching Bridge 56, Austey Wood can be seen to the right. Bridge 55 is a cantilever 'nick-bridge', allowing the towing rope to pass through when the horse crossed over. We too cross over to follow the towpath on the other side. Bridge 54, newer looking, comes next.

The second aqueduct now appears. This too was the work of William

Whitmore in 1813, and crosses the Stratford Road. Just before the beginning of the aqueduct take the steep path down to the road (unless you first wish to explore the wharf area just ahead). On the opposite side is the signboard to the Navigation Inn (the original Inn sign is on display by the entrance).

Cross this busy road very carefully and turn left along the Stratford Road (or right if coming out of the Navigation Inn) for the return into Wootton Wawen.

The third, and final water-mill is soon reached on the right, a magnificent building, from the late eighteenth century, operated by water from the River Alne, and retained in Wootton Pool. The original mill pond, and sluice gates, are still in existence.

An interesting coat of arms appears on the house opposite.

From the ballustraded bridge crossing the river, constructed by G. H. Capewell Hughes, of Wootton Hall in 1906, and beyond the waterfall, bulrushes and the beginnings of the osier beds and heronry, stretching some way to the north, are visible. An 1806 milestone set into the stone wall reads:

To London 100 miles
Birmingham 16

The Hall, built in 1687 by the 2nd Viscount Carington, was once the childhood home of a widow, a Mrs. Fitzherbert, who in 1785 became secretly married to the Prince of Wales, later George IV, only to be unscrupulously dropped from his company by 1803. More recent events concern the restoration work to the original pitched roof, which was ruined by a fire in 1941.

At the beginning of the driveway to Wootton Hall are the eighteenth century Lodge and huge iron gates. The Carington family coat of arms can be seen on the front of Wootton Hall. Behind the Hall, there are toilets, and a telephone, a dovecote, and one of the most unusual Post Offices in the country.

The X20 bus stop back to Birmingham or Stratford is just opposite the driveway to the Hall. For the car park and railway station, retrace your steps past restored seventeenth and eighteenth century cottages to the B4089, turning down beside the sixteenth century half-timbered Bulls Head.

17
Alcester and the River Arrow
by Martin Spink

From Alcester this is a circular walk taking in a stretch of the River Arrow and a crossing of the River Alne, going through the countryside around Oversley Castle and Oversley Wood, Haselor village and church, Great Alne and part of the Alne Hills, and passing near Coughton Court National Trust House and Spernall. (If you are intending to go inside the Court, which is a National Trust property, it would be wise to check beforehand on its opening times by telephoning 01789-400777.)

Distance: 14 miles (22.5 km), 11 miles (17.5 km) or 8 miles (13 km).
Maps: Landranger 150; Pathfinder 975/997.
Car Parking: Alcester: Main car park behind High Street reached by car from either Birmingham or Great Alne via School Road and then Moorfield Road (GR089575). Another free car park is at Bleachfield Street. To reach the church from the main shopping car park there are two alleys giving pedestrian access via the main high street.
Public Transport: Stratford Blue 213/208/228 (Redditch-Studley-Alcester-Stratford); Midland Red West 146/176 (Birmingham-Alcester-Evesham).
Start/Finish: Alcester (GR090574). From the car park or the bus stop walk to the centre of Alcester aiming for the Church of St Nicholas. The walk starts along Mill Lane where it joins High Street/Church Lane at the south-eastern corner of the churchyard.
Refreshments: Pubs in Alcester; Great Alne. Tea shops in Alcester. Coughton Court National Trust Property has a shop, tea shop and restaurant.
Shorter Variations: The main walk can be shortened to A) 8 miles by taking a short cut from Oversley Wood via Coughton Fields to Church Farm, visiting *en route* the Kinwarton Dovecote; or B) to 11 miles by omitting the northerly loop to Spernall.

G O SOUTHWARDS down Malt Mill Lane, now pedestrianised and attractively restored and marked with a waymark sign for the Heart of England Way, until you reach a wall and old lamp-post at the bottom. Here turn right and walk until you reach the end of the wall. Turn left and walk along a path on the right of a bank with the River Arrow on the left of the bank. You reach the main road, where there is another waymark sign for the Heart of England Way. Cross the main road and take the road opposite signposted Oversley Green.

Continue along this road with the River Arrow on your left and cross the bridge where the River Alne and River Arrow both meet.

Carry on to the next triangular junction, go right along Mill Lane and take the first road left, Primrose Lane. Cross the bridge over the A46(T), go over a stile and take the right hand footpath, still on the Heart of England Way, and up the side of a hill to Primrose Farm. Here you can look down on Alcester and see the Alne Hills in the distance.

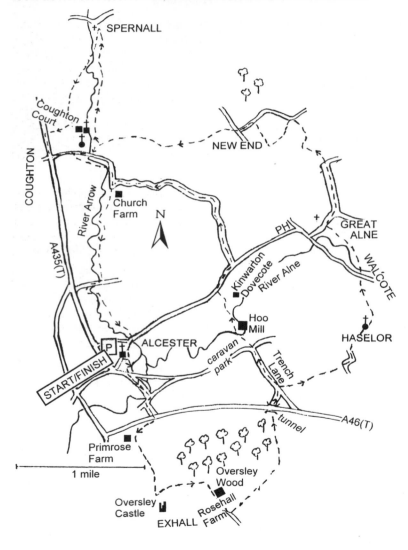

Bridge at the meeting of the Arrow and the Alne

Turn left just before Primrose Farm and walk along a track towards another hill on which Oversley Castle can be seen through the trees. (Ragley Hall can also be seen on your right across the field before this, on the other side of the valley.) Turn left at the next T-junction of tracks at the foot of Oversley Castle, now leaving the Heart of England Way, to arrive at the SW corner of Oversley Wood. Follow the blue arrow straight on (avoiding the left turn track back to Alcester). Walk just inside the south edge of the wood on a woodland trail. After 300 metres where the trail ends and you reach an open field, turn right going through two gates to pass Rose Hall Farm. Follow a lane to reach a road on the outskirts of the village of Exhall.

At this point you could visit this village and the church by turning right along the road. Exhall is an attractive village with a number of timber framed cottages. Parts of the well-kept church date back to the twelfth century and it contains two Elizabethan brass effigies.

Turn left at the road and after 40 paces go left through a gate marked Valley Farm and stay on this track for half a mile, going through two gates.

When the track splits into two in front of two adjacent gates go through the left hand one. Follow the right-hand hedge to the far right hand corner of the field and go through a small gate at the SE corner of Oversley Wood which you have now reached. Continue with Oversley Wood on your left hand side and a field and Alcocks Arbour on your right and pass a larger gate. Follow a track through another field until you reach a gate and stile and go over this and through a road tunnel under the A46(T) straight ahead of you. Follow the lane straight on (not left to Oversley Green), until you reach Trench Lane, the main road (the old A422).

This is the point at which the shorter walk A (8 miles) separates. For the longer walks now continue reading from ✱ on page 91.

Continuing on shorter walk A, turn left and walk *very carefully* along the road (there is a grassy verge on the left hand side, which should help you to avoid the busy traffic) and taking you northwards in the direction of Hoo Mill. Turn right at the next road junction signposted 'Haselor and Walcote', then turn almost immediately left down a narrow No Through Road towards Hoo Mill. After 200 metres the road starts to bend towards the right but instead of following it to Hoo Mill itself, take the footpath on the left of the road. Cross the footbridge over the River Alne, then walk straight ahead across the field, aiming for the far right-hand corner, alongside the river. On the right hand side you can look across the river and see Hoo Mill, which is private property, and a steep weir is visible from the bank from the days of the mill.

Further along the river where the river meets a fence there is a gate. Pass through it and go up the lane which bends to the right at a house. Continue to the triangular junction and turn right, then pass by the Glebe Farm main entrance and walk along the road alongside a Tudor style brick and wood barn. Immediately at the end of the barn there is a door within a brick arch and this is the entrance to Glebe Farm where you can, if you wish, obtain the key to the Kinwarton Dovecote which you can shortly visit.

Carry on past the church of Saint Mary the Virgin, Kinwarton, to the gate in front of the Kinwarton Dovecote now owned by the National Trust. The Dovecote can be visited after going through this gate, going inside it using the key obtained from Glebe Farm. Beyond the Dovecote is a fine moat that you may also care to visit.

Return back to the gate at the entrance to the Dovecote field, *remembering to return the key to Glebe Farm if you have borrowed it*. On the right of this gate (with your back to the Dovecote) is another metal gate. Go through this and walk straight across the field (NNW) to another gate by a large oak tree. Go through this gate and cross the main road onto the pavement, then go right and walk 175 metres to reach a junction with a minor road signposted 'Coughton 2 miles via ford'. Turn left and walk down this quiet country lane for a mile and a half, passing Coughton Fields Farm on the right, then a house on the right, to reach

Church Farm on the left. (Church Farm is hidden by trees and so is easily missed.)

Here, at Church Farm, the shorter walk A rejoins the main walk. Just at the right of the entrance to Church Farm is a waymarked stile. Reach it and now continue reading from ◉ on page 95.

✳ Continuing the main walk, at Trench Lane cross the road carefully, turn left, and walk 40 paces which should bring you to a stile beside a double gate. Go over the stile, turn right and walk along the right hand side of the field with a hedge on your right, following the waymarked route.

Reaching a double gate on your right go through this (not the one straight ahead) and walk with the hedge on your left. Approaching the next pair of gates on the left cross back to walk with the hedge now on your right, passing through another pair of gates straight ahead. Carry on forward and just before reaching a copse join a path coming in left from an old ruin (marked Upton Barn on the Pathfinder map) and go right through yet another pair of gates. Turn left and walk along a farm track until it reaches a road at a bend. Follow the road straight ahead, then swing left into Haselor.

Continue straight along the road using the pavement on the left hand side. Just after the pavement rises above the road turn right down steps, and cross the road opposite the village stocks. Go through the gate above them which is the entrance to the parish church of St. Mary and All

Approaching Haselor Church

91

Saints, parts of which date back to the eleventh century. Follow a tarmac path first down a hill and through a gate, then up to the church itself. It is an interesting church and a distinctive landmark, being at the top of its own hill which suggests that it was originally a pagan site. The uneven ground around the church is thought to be due to the foundations of buildings abandoned after the Black Death. You have a good view across the Alne valley to the Alne Hills. In the NW corner of the graveyard one of the gravestones, to two former occupants of Hoo Mill, is made from a millstone. In the church entrance you could get twenty ramblers sheltering from the rain!

Leave the churchyard by the far kissing gate and walk down a path, passing the remains of what is probably the original village cross destroyed by Government order at the time of the Reformation. Reach a road and a 1953 Coronation Bench on the outskirts of Walcote. Cross the road with the large house opposite on the right, and go over the waymarked stile on the left of the house.

Walk along the right hand edge of the field and cross the next stile, then walk along the right hand edge of the next field and cross a double stile, then continue in the same direction to a small gate just above a road. Go down steps to arrive rather dangerously and unexpectedly on a bend in a road without pavement. (Across the road on your right are two rushing weirs on the River Alne.) Cross the road, turn left and after a few yards turn right to go across a footbridge over the river. You are now on an island in the River Alne.

Continue straight ahead after the bridge, crossing a field and following a track which eventually bears left where you walk across the lawn in front of you, passing tennis courts on your left, towards the old Alne Mill, now a dwelling place of several apartments. Walk towards the left hand or patio end, passing a waymark sign on a telegraph pole. Pass the patio end of the mill and then immediately turn right down the path along its side (there is a waymark sign on a rock on the ground). (*Do not turn left over their small garden footbridge*). Continue forward past the mill, noting the remains of the old mill mechanisms on your left, to reach the drive where you turn left to pass by the right side of a gate.

From the drive gate walk straight ahead down the drive (which itself goes to Great Alne) for 90 paces. This should bring you just past a tree where there is a small stile to watch out for on the left hand fence. Go over this into the field and cross the field diagonally (approximately NW) to the hedge opposite to where there is a kissing gate. Go through this and cross the next field in the same direction as you have been going, aiming diagonally to the right to cut off the right hand corner of the field (approximately in the direction of Great Alne church which you may be able to see through the trees).

Next, cross the track of the old dismantled railway line, which once linked Alcester and Stratford, then go through the gate to the next field. From this gate go diagonally to the left heading towards a large tree and avoiding the stables and gate straight ahead. Just past a hedge corner on the right of the tree is a stile. Cross this and walk forward (west) in the direction of the red brick telephone exchange building (somewhat hidden by trees in the summer) passing it on your left and go through a kissing gate in the corner of the field to arrive at the main road in Great Alne.

If you turn left here and follow the main road in the direction of Alcester you reach the Mother Huff Cap pub (see also page 82) after about 500 metres, a useful midpoint break in the walk.

Otherwise cross the road and turn right, and walk towards the overhanging chestnut tree where there is some parking space. On the right of the tree is a path waymarked to the church at Great Alne. This is also an attractive church and location and surrounded by a small graveyard. There is no public right of way through the church but if you wish to visit it take this path.

To avoid returning by the same route you can take the kissing gate at the far right hand side of the church, cross part of a field with a hedge on the right, then go through a second kissing gate and along a hedged path followed by an alley to reach Park Lane where you turn left to rejoin the walk.

From the chestnut tree continue walking easterly about 200-250 metres and turn left at the first tarmac road signposted Park Lane. Follow this road straight (not to Maudslay) for just under a kilometre. At the point when the road bends sharply right under a large tree, becoming a private road to Alne Park, go straight ahead over a gate and continue in the same direction across the field, parallel to the wire fence on your right. The Severn Trent water board has a presence on the hill on the left.

Ahead you are walking towards trees into a narrowing valley and as you reach the trees do not go through the gate straight ahead or up to the right but climb up the steep left bank watching out for a waymark sign on a large tree in front of a stile, which you cross. Follow the field edge on the right hand side, cross a stile and turn right as a sign indicates and go along the edge of a larger field. Turn left at the field corner and go all the way along this right hand field edge to the far right corner where there is a stile under a large tree.

Go over the stile and cross the next field diagonally left (NNW) to arrive at another stile at a bend on a minor road. Turn left after the stile and after 35 paces along the road cross another stile on the left, marked

Heart of England Way, by the entrance to Dingwell Cottage. Now follow the left side of the field past the house and down a hill to a gate for a view of the Alne Valley with Oversley Wood in the distance. Cross the stile and descend across the field diagonally left to another stile at a farm track. Cross this stile, turn right and walk along this track.

After about 100 metres pass a house on the left, then after almost another 100 metres look out for an easily missed stile on the left – but don't go over it. A couple of paces past this go through a gap in the hedge on the right and follow the right hand field boundary for about 400 metres to come out on a minor road. Turn left and walk to the T-junction at New End. Turn right at the T-junction and walk about 40-50 paces along the main road passing some houses. After the last house on the left turn left along a track and follow this for about 2 km.

If you now wish to follow the shorter walk B go through a gate at the end of the track to arrive at a minor road where it crosses the River Arrow at a ford. Turn right to cross the footbridge by the ford, then walk a few minutes up the road to Coughton Court Presbytery, which is at the first right-hand road junction where a sign indicates the road is for Coughton Court coaches only. Now read from ✪ on page 95

Continuing along the full walk: almost at the end of the track, about 100 metres before the track goes through a gate and trees, look out for a waymarked stile over to the left. From this a faint path crosses the track at right angles. Turn right along this path, going towards trees by the River Arrow.

By the first gate, cross the stile, then walk northwards towards the nearest of many large oak trees and follow the posts along the left side of this small patch of trees. The rear of Coughton Court can be seen on your left across the River Arrow. Go through a small gate at the next fence, then follow the track through the next field. Cross a wooden footbridge to the next field, then follow the path forward across the field, soon passing alongside the River Arrow. Cross a ditch at a gap in a fence and continue forward. Go through the gap in the next fence, swing very slightly right to meet a meander of the river and follow this to reach another fence, at the other end of which are the buildings of Lower Spernall Farm. Cross this fence using a stile at the River Arrow end.

Go straight ahead across a large field. A short way along on the left is the footbridge which is the return route but at the far side of the field is Spernall church and rectory. Cross the field to the churchyard.

The former church of St Leonard's, Spernall is now owned by the Ancient Monuments Society and is boarded up. The first rector was recorded in 1270 but church origins probably are twelfth century. The Chancel was rebuilt in 1844. It is now closed for worship but is being preserved by the society because of its historic interest. The old rectory is private property, and is located just behind the church.

After visiting the church return across the field to the footbridge and cross the River Arrow. Walk across the next field, with the River Arrow and trees on the left, to reach the end of this field, then cross a double stile. In the next field go diagonally right (SW) to a gate in the far right hand corner by three oaks. Coughton Court is now in view to the south.

Go through the gate, then diagonally right to cut off the next field corner and walk with the hedge and some magnificent oaks on your right towards Coughton Court. At the far corner is a west facing stile: turn right to cross it. Walk alongside the fence on your right to another stile ahead. Cross it then walk diagonally WSW across to the far side of a field aiming for the left side of a house, somewhat hidden behind trees and by the height of the field.

Cross the stile beside a gate at the house and walk along the drive to the main road. Turn left and walk along the main road, passing by the main car entrance to Coughton Court and until you reach a crossroads. Turn left along Coughton Fields Lane opposite the old post office and tea room. After 300 metres you reach the south entrance of Coughton Court by the Presbytery (Coughton Court coaches only).

✪ (*The shorter walk B rejoins the main walk here.*) Here, if it is open, is an opportunity to visit Coughton Court (National Trust), a historic stately home and home of the Throckmorton family from the 1400s to the present century, featuring a house and grounds, a short riverside walk, a shop, and refreshment facilities. To reach it go past the coaches sign at the gate and walk along the drive to the front of the main building. Then return to this road junction after the visit.

To continue the walk go through the metal kissing gate which is on the opposite side of the road to the Coughton Court turning. Two public footpaths are signposted from this metal kissing gate. Take the one going diagonally to the left, roughly parallel to the hedge, back towards the River Arrow. Go under a power line, and keeping straight reach and go through a kissing gate which is adjacent to a gate. Now follow a grassy track to another footbridge crossing the River Arrow and turn right onto a quiet minor road.

Continue along this road past two houses on the left. After about 200 metres past the houses the road bends to the left and at the first farm entrance on the right, Church Farm, just behind the hedge on the right there is a waymarked stile.

◉ (*The shorter walk A rejoins the main walk here.*) From the stile there is a view ahead with Oversley Wood on the skyline and the final stretch of the walk along the River Arrow to Alcester in between. Go over the stile and then cross the field in front of you, aiming for the river on the far right-hand side of the field where a waymark sign directs you along a riverside path, the river on your right.

Continue following the path alongside the river, first bending to the left, then passing a weir with some industrial land on the opposite bank, soon reaching a waymark sign beside a gate indicating a more direct route to the left than along the river.

Follow this waymarked route, cross a stile (ignoring another immediately before this on the right) and continue briefly with the river on the right. Just after this, where the path splits, ignore the river path to the right but swing left, soon, however, picking up the river again and entering the edge of the Arden Forest Industrial Estate.

Here join a riverside gravel path, bearing left along it when you reach a low bridge. It takes you up to the road bridge. Cross the road, turn right and walk along the pavement about 50 metres, crossing the river. Turn left down steps onto a landscaped path and go right almost straightaway to follow the river along the right bank until you reach the next bridge. Cross back to the original side of the river at this bridge. Immediately turn right passing picnic chairs and a market garden and entering a public park. Keep the river on your right and soon join a track coming in from the left.

Briefly follow this straight track for about 20 metres but then bear right, leaving it to follow a path along the trees on your right on entering a recreation ground. After 35 metres from the end of the straight track ignore the next path on the right which takes you closer to the river but which, due to a steep bank and tree roots, is effectively a path cul de sac. However, after 80 metres, as the recreation ground widens into two football fields and just before passing the first goal post, you can take a right-hand path which will take you close to the river to follow its meanders and then return you back to the first football field. Turn right and follow the edge of the trees, then the riverbank, to the end of the second football field.

Join up with the track at the end of the football field. At the end of the track you will pass a Sports Hall and reach the Kinwarton road where you turn right to cross the River Arrow once more. 300 metres further on the road joins the High Street at Alcester church and you are at the end of the walk.

18
A Shakespeare Round
by Peter Groves

The Stratford-upon-Avon Canal, the River Avon and the Shottery Brook link together many historic sites that are associated with our greatest playwright. This walk combines their watersides with field paths to provide a historical exploration that can be followed as a single 21 km walk or be split into two sections, of 12 km and 11 km.

Distances: 13 miles (21 km), 7½ miles (12 km), or 6¾ miles (11 km).
Maps: Landranger 151; Pathfinder 997.
Car Parking: Several car parks in Stratford.
Public Transport: Stagecoach service X20 Birmingham/Stratford; BR to Stratford.
Start/Finish: Bancroft Gardens, Stratford-upon-Avon (GR204548)
Refreshments: Inns in Wilmcote, Shottery and Stratford; teashops in Shottery and Stratford.
Shorter Walks: The first shorter section starts, together with the main walk, in Stratford and separates from it at Shottery from where there is by a regular local bus service to Stratford (Stratford Blue Shuttle). The second shorter section starts from Shottery. For this section start reading from ✱ on page 101.

WE START, appropriately, at the Shakespeare Memorial in the Bancroft Gardens. Unveiled in 1888, the memorial was moved here from the Theatre Gardens in 1933. The imposing figure of Shakespeare is surrounded by four characters from his plays that illustrate history (Prince Hal), philosophy (Hamlet), tragedy (Lady Macbeth) and comedy (Falstaff).

From here, with your back to the Tourist Office and the road, go left round the canal basin. The Stratford-upon-Avon Canal was opened to the Avon in 1816 having been built on a tight budget and after many delays, largely due to economic problems in the country resulting from the Napoleonic wars. By the 1930s trade on the canal had ceased and it was semi-derelict for several years. Attempts were made to have it dismantled but through the efforts of the National Trust it was restored and reopened in 1964. It links to the Birmingham & Worcester Canal and to the Grand Union Canal at Lapworth, and to the River Avon here at Stratford. It was particularly important for the transport of coal from Midlands collieries.

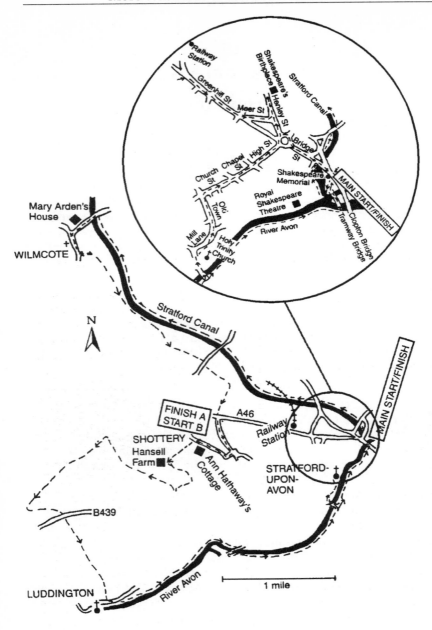

Cross the bridge at the Barge Lock (No. 56, and the last lock on the canal) noting the modestly clad statue at the side of the bridge. On the bridge a plaque records details of the canal restoration. Ahead you can see the Royal Shakespeare Theatre. This dates from 1932 and replaced an earlier theatre opened in 1879 which was destroyed by fire in 1926.

From the bridge go right and around the canal basin, soon passing the now blocked off canal link to the original basin. On the site of this there is an attractive modern sculpture celebrating the 800th anniversary of the granting of market rights to the town by Richard I. Go under road bridge 69 and immediately walk along an attractive stretch of the Stratford- upon-Avon Canal, crossing to the other side at bridge 68.

We are now going to follow the Stratford Canal for 5 km, passing sixteen locks, some closely spaced, that take the canal up the Birmingham plateau. Look out for some split bridges – constructed in two pieces with a gap in the centre to allow the towrope to pass through. This is a much cheaper form of construction than the more common brick-built bridge, a consequence of the financial difficulties that faced the company.

You will soon pass under two railway bridges, one carrying a dismantled line, the other the Stratford-Birmingham line. Immediately after these your taste buds may be activated by the delicious odours emanating from the food factory that you pass on the right! At bridge 63 look out for the large house with its fine set of high chimneys. Lock

Wilmcote. Mary Arden's House

99

40 is accompanied by a former lock keeper's cottage: on the wall is some very interesting information about the cottage.

Leave the canal at the concrete bridge following split bridge 60 (i.e. no. 59, although it has no number on it) and walk up to the road. Turn right over the bridge into Wilmcote, soon passing Mary Arden's House on the right. The house belonged to the family of Shakespeare's mother, the Ardens, who lived here in the sixteenth century. It remained a working farm until 1930 and retains much of the character that it would have had in Shakespeare's time. Look out for some falcons in the garden just past the house.

After admiring, and perhaps visiting, the house continue forward to the T-junction where the Mary Arden Inn faces you and turn left along Church Road. (Another pub, the Mason's Arms is to the right.) You soon reach the Church of St Andrew, built in 1840, and very attractively decorated inside, particularly in the sanctuary with biblical scenes and texts painted on zinc plates in the 1870s by a former incumbent.

After about a further 200 metres turn left along Manor Drive, then as the road goes into a housing estate go left over a stile beside a gate. Follow the main track which, after about 50 metres, swings to the right and leads back to the Stratford Canal. However, just before reaching the canal and split bridge 60 turn off to the right and walk with a hedge on the left, through which you will get occasional glimpses of the canal.

At the end of the very long field, where the hedge swings round to the right, go through an easily-missed gap in the hedge and cross a footbridge with a stile. Continue forward, still with the canal on your left, and walk through three fields, in the third field passing Copham's Hill Farm on your right. At the end of the third field turn right, walking with a hedge on the left and now leaving the canal. Cross a stile and reach a concrete farm drive, along which go left. Cross the busy A46(T) *very carefully*, go through the metal kissing gate opposite and down the concrete track and through another kissing gate.

Reaching a minor road cross this, turn right and walk forward for about 30 metres, then turn left along a tarmac footpath signed Stratford ¾. Continue forward through a new housing estate, noting the ornithological character of the roads! Cross a road and continue forward along the tarmac path, swinging right. Meeting a crossing path turn left along this with a wall on your right.

Continue with a fence on the left and swing right to reach a road. Turn left along this and then right to walk with the Shottery Brook over to your left. When the path swings right go forward over a grassed area to reach a road that crosses the brook. Cross the road and walk along the surfaced path to join a road and continue forward along Heather Close.

Shottery. Anne Hathaway's Cottage

When the Close swings right go down to the main road. Cross the road carefully and turn left, then right along Church Lane, signed 'Anne Hathaway's Cottage. ½ mile'. After about 500 metres, just before a road junction, you will see on the right steps leading to a gate to Anne Hathaway's cottage.

However, if at this stage you are in need of refreshment 'The Bell' is nearby – cross the road ahead and walk forward a short distance.

Continuing, go up the steps, through a gate and along a path, over the Shottery Brook and cross the road to reach the cottage. It was, like Mary Arden's house, originally a farmhouse and was the home until 1892 of many generations of the Hathaway family. Anne Hathaway married William Shakespeare, probably in 1582 or 1583. Many of the furnishings in the cottage belonged to the Hathaway family and it possesses the genuine atmosphere of an Elizabethan farmhouse. The cottage garden with its adjoining orchard is a delight. To the right of the cottage is 'The Thatch' restaurant.

For the shorter walk now continue reading from ❂ on page 105. Alternatively you can take a Stratford Blue Shuttle bus back into Stratford.

✴ Continuing with the longer walk (or starting the second shorter walk), after leaving the cottage turn left (or turn right if, on the longer walk, you do not go into the cottage) and walk along the road for about 300 metres and then turn left along a surfaced right of way, signed Hansell Farm. At the top of the incline, 10 metres before the farm, go through a kissing gate on the left and walk with a fence on the right. Go through a wicket gate to find a fine sundial, erected to the memory of a local farmer.

Bearing slightly left, go down the field and swing right to enter a coppice, noting the fine views ahead. Emerge from the coppice, having just ignored a crossing path. Turn right and walk with the coppice on the right for about 300 metres to reach a T-junction of paths. Here turn right and follow the path for about 1½ kilometres. Just past the turn, in a dell to the right, are the remains of a wartime shooting range.

About 100 metres after crossing a stiled footbridge (where ignore a path to the right) turn left to cross a stile beside a gate. Follow the path with a hedge on the right through two fields, ignoring a path going off to the right in the first field. Reaching Drayton Farm on the right cross a stile and walk for about 75 metres, cross another stile on the right and go diagonally across to a third stile. Over this go diagonally left (SW) passing under power lines to reach and cross a gate stile in the far left corner of the field, immediately crossing a footbridge.

Having passed to the right of a hedge now walk through three fields, keeping a brook on your left. Almost at the end of the third field turn left and cross a footbridge through the hedge and walk along a track, passing a wooded area on the left. Cross a stile beside a gate, then another immediately on the right and go diagonally across a field, aiming just to the left of the furthermost power pole. Cross a stile and go through an area of young woodland to reach the B439, via a stile and footbridge.

Cross the road *very carefully* and take the path immediately opposite. Walk with a hedge on the right, passing an industrial centre on the left and very soon going through a gate. Continue, still with the hedge on the right, through seven fields. In the third field the path crosses to the right-hand side of the hedge but, on approaching an orchard, reverts to the left-hand side. It crosses a bridge over a dismantled railway and soon passes a pool on the right.

Leave the final field through a gate in the far right corner and go along the driveway of a house and on to the road in Luddington. Passing an attractive thatched cottage turn left and after about 100 metres take the footpath on the right. Walk diagonally across the field to a stile at the end of a row of trees. Cross this and continue diagonally forward to reach and turn left along the River Avon to walk for about four kilometres back to Stratford-upon-Avon. The far bank of the river is marked for much of the way by pollarded willows.

At one stage you will find yourself walking through the gardens of a number of houses – but don't worry, you are still on a public footpath! A few years ago an attempt was made to close this section of path, which would have meant an unwelcome diversion along a road. However, the proposal was opposed by the Ramblers' Association and was eventually dropped. After several ascents and descents of steps you will cross a footbridge and reach an open field again. Ahead can be seen the spire of Holy Trinity Church in Stratford.

On reaching the steel-girdered bridge of another dismantled railway Stratford Racecourse is on the left. Go under the bridge and take the path on the left (passing a picnic area on your right) that will take you up the embankment to the old line. This is now 'The Greenway', a five mile walkway/cycleway/bridleway originally the Honeybourne Railway, built in 1859 and closed in 1976. Turn left and walk over the bridge, trusting that the supports are less corroded than the girders on your right! About 100 m after crossing the bridge go down the slope on the left, cross a stile, turn left and walk towards Stratford along the Avon Walkway.

Continue through fields until steps take you into a wooded area with the River Avon below you on the left. Steps will then take you down to one of the new locks which, constructed in the period 1969-1974, made the navigation of the River Avon once again possible. Continue along the riverside path until you reach and pass under the bridge that carries the A4390 over the river.

Here you have a choice – to continue with the Shakespeare theme or with the waterside theme. If you would like to return into the town along the river now continue reading from ◉ on page 105.

However, to visit Shakespeare's birthplace and his tomb and to see some of old Stratford cross the river by the footbridge, turn right and walk along the tarmac path between a hedge and a wall to join the road and go into the churchyard of Holy Trinity Church. This is the church where Shakespeare was baptised, married and buried, and contains many fascinating features that are fully described in the guide that you can buy inside the church. Shakespeare's tomb is, of course, a major attraction and to visit it requires a contribution to the restoration fund. Even if you don't go into the church do go and see the thirteenth century sanctuary doorknocker on the inner door to the main church entrance. Reaching this, in days past, would give any fugitive from justice protection for thirty-seven days.

From the main entrance take the path forward through the churchyard. This is bordered by lime trees, twelve on the right and eleven on the left. The twelve represent the twelve tribes of Israel, the eleven the twelve apostles but with Judas Iscariot missing. However, behind the first gap is a twelfth tree representing St Mathias who took the place of Judas Iscariot. A duplicate set of young trees, planted 1993/94, will replace the older ones when they have to be felled. The flagstones along the avenue mark some family vaults.

On leaving the churchyard turn right, then swing left into Stratford

Old Town. You will pass some sixteenth century cottages followed by Hall's Croft, also sixteenth century and carefully restored by the Shakespeare Birthplace Trust. It was the residence of John Hall, an eminent physician who married Shakespeare's daughter Susanna in 1607. Hall's Croft, with rooms furnished in the style of the period, houses a variety of items that illustrate medical practice in Dr Hall's time.

Turn right into Church Street to pass on the right the Windmill Inn which has been licensed for some three hundred and fifty years. Opposite is Mason Croft which, as a plaque proclaims, was the home of Marie Corelli, a popular novelist who lived here from 1901 to 1924.

A little further, on the right, you will pass a row of eleven fifteenth century almshouses, little changed since Shakespeare's time. Beyond is the entrance to the Grammar School, also fifteenth century. It is thought that Shakespeare was probably a pupil here.

At the corner of Church Street and Chapel Lane is the medieval Guild Chapel which is well worth a visit. Over the chancel arch is the remains of a famous medieval wall painting, *The Day of Judgement*, in which figures on the right are welcomed into heaven by St Peter whereas, on the left, devils hurl sinners into a fiery cauldron!

Continue along Church Street to pass, on the left, the Falcon Hotel dating back to around 1500. On the right was New Place where Shakespeare lived from 1610 until his death there in 1616. It was demolished in the last century and today only the foundations and the garden remain. Beside the site is Nash's House, Stratford's local history museum and once the home of Shakespeare's grand-daughter Elizabeth Hall.

Continuing along Chapel Street you will pass the Shakespeare Hotel, dating from 1637, and, on the left, the Midland Bank carrying a frieze illustrating scenes from Shakespeare's plays. Opposite, on the corner with Sheep Street is the Town Hall, notable for its many associations with the actor, David Garrick, and carrying the faded inscription 'GOD SAVE THE KING'.

Continue forward along High Street to pass some fine Tudor buildings including the Garrick Inn and Harvard House on the left. Keep on the left-hand side of the road and cross Wood Street to reach Henley Street and turn left to Shakespeare's birthplace. Although the precise date when this was built is not known John Shakespeare, William's father, was living here in 1552 and carrying on his trade as a glover and wool dealer. The building has been maintained and is furnished as authentically as possible. You may wish to spend any remaining time here, immersing yourself in its atmosphere (though probably accompanied by countless numbers of tourists!). Next door is the Shakespeare Centre with even more memorabilia.

Now, to return to the start of the walk retrace your steps back along Henley Street and continue along Bridge Street to reach the Bancroft Gardens.

◉ Following the waterside theme continue along the riverside path back into Stratford. You soon pass an attractive weir and then reach the Colin P Witter Lock with Holy Trinity Church on the opposite side of the river. Having passed Stratford Boat Club cross the river by the Tramway Bridge. Now a footbridge, this originally carried a horse-drawn tramway that linked the canal and river to Shipston-on-Stour and Moreton-in-Marsh. Across to the right is the Clopton Bridge which, until the recent building of a relief road, carried the A34. It was built in the fifteenth century and that its fourteen arches have survived so much modern traffic is a great tribute to its sound construction. It is named after its builder, Sir Hugh Clopton, a native of Stratford who was Lord Mayor of London in 1492 and a generous benefactor to his home town. On an island in the river you will see the N.R.A. Nature Reserve. Just beyond you will pass one of the tramway wagons on an original length of track, and you are then back at your starting point.

○ *Shorter walk.*

Turn right from the cottage (or left if you did not visit the cottage) and walk along the road which soon reaches a crossroads. Here continue forward and, when the road very shortly swings right, walk ahead along Tavern Lane passing a bus stop and a thatched cottage. Reaching Bramley House the path, signed 'Stratford, Shakespeare's Birthplace', continues forward between a wall and a fence with a sports field on the left. At a cross-paths turn left signed 'Market Place, Shakespeare's Birthplace'. Go past a children's play area and a school. Reaching a road cross this, go left a few metres and turn right along the tarmacked footpath. At a Y-junction in the path turn right to reach Alcester Road.

If you have travelled by train and wish to finish here a left turn will bring you to the railway station. But for a visit to Shakespeare's birthplace and to return to the starting point in Bancroft Gardens turn right, go over Arden Street and along Greenhill Street, then left along Meer Street. This will bring you to Henley Street with Shakespeare's birthplace and the Shakespeare Centre to the left, both of which are well worth a visit. A turn to the right will take you into Bridge Street and a short walk along here will return you to the start.

Acknowledgement: *In preparing this walk I have made use of an excellent little book 'Exploring Stratford: A Guided Tour' by Enid Colston (Meridian Books). It has taught me a great deal about Shakespeare and shown me much that I might otherwise have missed.*

Index

106